MW00888153

How to Be A Great Teacher
Create the Flow of Joy and Success in Your Classroom

WYNN GODBOLD

How to Be a Great Teacher: Create the Flow of Joy and Success in Your Classroom
By Wynn Godbold

Bee Sharp LLC
4504 Boxwood Street
Myrtle Beach, SC 29577

On the web: www.HowtoBeaGreatTeacher.com or
www.BeeSharp.us

Bulk ordering is available for schools, school districts, colleges, universities, and other institutions. Contact info@BeeSharp.us for information.

Cover design by Blue Sun Studio, Inc.

ISBN-13: 9781492399209

ISBN-10: 1492399205

Go confidently in the direction of your dreams. Live the life you have imagined.
Henry David Thoreau

Contents

Preface

MY STORY OF WHY

*W*hen my momma was living, she used to say that I was my favorite subject. Despite the fact that she was right, I swear this time when I share my story it is for *your* benefit, not mine. I promise. It's important to know people's stories. When I hear someone's story, I imagine myself enjoying his or her successes. I try to learn from his or her mistakes. That part doesn't always work out, but I try. Knowing other people's stories also helps us understand each other and form a context for the ideas we share. It's much easier to accept crazy when you know where it came from.

In this light, here is my story. Here is the background that caused me to dispel the current idea of what makes a good teacher and propose a new and better paradigm: the paradigm of the great fountain teacher.

Idealism and Feeling Overwhelmed

I began my teaching career in a Title I school located in the farthest reaches of my county school district. If you're not aware, Title I schools serve students who are economically disadvantaged or at risk for failing to meet standards. These schools easily rank as some of the most challenging environments in which you'll ever teach. I chose to apply to this school because I was completely filled with optimism, excitement, and plenty of idealism. Feel free to interpret that as young, dumb, and starry-eyed.

My particular Title I school was surrounded by corn, cotton, and tobacco fields. The forty-five minute drive from home to school each morning transported me from a place I knew and loved to hell on Earth. It did not take long for my idealism to turn to feeling overwhelmed. I realized quickly that the class I had been given to teach was full of living, breathing, talking, running, interrupting, and disadvantaged first-graders. Clearly, teaching these children would not be as easy or as much fun as the class of stuffed animals I had taught in my backyard schoolhouse when I was in third grade. I'll spare you the gory details of my first year teaching. I'm sure you have a first-year teaching story of your own to reflect upon.

With the help and support of some fantastic colleagues during that tumultuous first year, I eventually caught my stride. For a short period of time, I kept my head above water. I thought I could even see a light signaling the shore. I was going to survive!

Just when I thought my dream of being a teacher really might work out, my principal began sharing, in rather lengthy meetings after school, about this new thing called "No Child Left Behind."

Anger

As you might imagine or have even experienced for yourself, I quickly became disillusioned with my purpose as teacher in the classroom. Standardized testing and scores became more important than children. I felt that my existence in the classroom was simply about producing scores, not growing children. Honestly, I got ticked off about that. I spent some time lingering in anger. Grrr.

Awakening

Then it happened. I became fed up with my anger. This was the beginning of my awakening. I started questioning everything—first the challenges outside of me and then the challenges on the inside. At one point I remember thinking to myself, "Hold on a minute, this anger is not helping. The stuff you're mad about (testing/scores/the crushing blow to your dream of changing the world) is not going anywhere. If you're going to stay in this classroom, if you're going to love kids and impact lives the way you dreamed of doing since you were in the third grade, playing school all summer long in your backyard schoolhouse, you've got to reconcile your passion with the constraints of the times. You must find the joy within." Talk about an awakening!

Joy

You may be tempted to think that my awakening was a one-day epiphany and, *bang*, I had it; au contraire. In fact, that moment was only the beginning. The journey to joy took time, commitment, recognition, and recommitment. Getting to the point in my life where I could authentically teach with joy was a process. Developing true joy in contrast to experiencing fleeting moments of happiness is a process.

The Long Haul

I'm not sure there's any feeling worse in life than the one that has you believing that you are a complete failure at the one thing you were called by God to do. After my first year teaching, this was my fear. I questioned myself repeatedly, "How could I have gotten this so wrong?" I had always wanted to be a teacher, but I was miserable, and I believed I stunk at teaching. I was embarrassed and ashamed to admit this to anyone. There I was, struggling in my dream job.

I was not a quitter, and, honestly, I was at a loss as to what I would do if not teaching. I requested and received a transfer to a school much closer to home and returned to the classroom the following year. I did a great deal of soul-searching. I watched videos by the teacher-motivator Harry Wong. I read his book and set out a new plan, keeping in mind all the things that went wrong in the first year. I studied my behavior. I listened to other teachers.

That's when I began to hear it. There were other teachers, women I respected and wanted to be like, who were showing signs of concern. They were having conversations about children, learning, and testing. I joined in. The struggles became more apparent and more widespread. Everyone in my school seemed to be jumping on the bandwagon. This made me feel like one of them. I was no longer alone. The problem was we did a lot of complaining. The mutual griping was not sustainable, and frankly, it was not particularly productive. It never is. This camaraderie, however, convinced me that I could hang in there.

We Were Not Alone

I continued several years with this group of teachers. I enjoyed fleeting moments of happiness, but the central issue of being the excellent teacher, the one I had dreamed of being, was still out for debate. I attempted to resolve my conflicts about my teaching by signing up for special duties and doing the one thing I had complete confidence in my ability to do: take classes. I began and completed the course-work required to obtain my certification as an elementary school principal. I applied, was accepted into, and worked in a teacher mentoring program funded by a special state grant. Despite my best efforts to mask my uncertainties, my rise to leadership did not solve my internal conflict between my desire to be a great teacher and my feelings of inadequacy surrounding my daily practices. Leadership did, however, expose me to more teachers throughout my school district.

When I started working all over my county, I realized my former colleagues and I were not alone. In fact, instead of just being out of congruence with our ideas about great teaching, more and more I found teachers who were overwhelmed, burned out, and frustrated. In my infinite wisdom, I jumped to the immediate conclusion that our superintendent must be the most horrible person in the entire world to ruin the lives of so many teachers. I was sure of it. For the record, she wasn't! But who else was I to blame?

Thank God for Summertime

Even in light of my false conclusion I was able to continue teaching year after year, counting the days of school until summer would arrive. After enjoying a few of my summer breaks on the shore and in the water parks of Myrtle Beach, an opportunity to make some summer money fell into my lap. Since it was not a waitressing job, I accepted. (Note to all the waitresses reading and in the world: I love you. I understand you. I was one of you for many years before teaching. I do not desire to ever do your work again. It is hard. God bless you.)

McGraw-Hill, the publishing company, hired me to travel the state of South Carolina and provide professional development to teachers who were using one of their programs. It was great fun. I realized in that summer that I have a gift for inspiring and empowering teachers. During this time, I also discovered that the state was filled with teachers who were overwhelmed, burned out, and frustrated. At that point, I had another epiphany. I realized, "Wow, it's not just me. It's not just my friends. It's not my district. Being overwhelmed, burned out, and frustrated exists everywhere in my state." From this I concluded that the trouble must be somewhere in our state house. Perhaps our governor was the problem.

The point is that I could see these feelings of being overwhelmed, frustrated, and burned out pushing teachers into dissatisfaction, early retirement, and anger of epic proportions. I believed we were doomed, but I didn't know what to do.

As the cycle of education goes, summer ended quick as a wink. I was back in my classroom, bothered by my discovery, but working full tilt with my students, too busy to change the state of South Carolina.

It Got Even Bigger

What started out as a lonely journey of self-doubt was now as big as South Carolina. I knew I was not alone, but I still felt helpless. I had not solved anything. I was filling voids with more responsibilities and still coming up empty and doubtful about my role as a great teacher.

Fast-forward to the following summer. McGraw-Hill began sending me all over the country to work with teachers. I'll give you three guesses to figure out what I found as I travelled. You probably got it right on the first guess: I found teachers everywhere who were overwhelmed, frustrated, and feeling burned out. Do you recognize the theme? Teachers were also dealing with loads of things that were negatively impacting their ability to be in their classrooms authentically loving kids, joyfully teaching, and achieving loads of success. The saddest part was many of these teachers were like me. They had dreamed of being a life-changing teacher since the time they were children. My guess is that if you chose this book, you share the same dream—and the same frustrations.

Teachers everywhere feel the way you feel. You are not alone. Feeling overwhelmed, burned out, and frustrated comes from the demands of testing but also from mandated budget restrictions, parents who either care too much or don't care enough, lack of administrative support, an overabundance of paperwork, standards, scripted curriculums, and more. What we set out to do—change children's lives—gets lost in the shuffle.

In addition, education is constant fodder for politicians and the media. Add in a few of our colleagues who do incredibly stupid things such as having sex with students, and you can quickly lose heart.

But There Is a Light!

After my national travels exposed the magnitude of the problem to me, I began to get more serious about discovering a solution. I let go of many of my leadership responsibilities and began to focus intently on how to fix my problem. Interestingly, I discovered the solution was inside of me. I did not need to fill my voids and spaces of uncertainty with more responsibilities. I needed to develop a clear vision of what I believed.

As I told you at the beginning of my story, this journey to joyful teaching was a process. It took years for me to realize how to be a great teacher. Then it required time, practice, and patience to live up to this ideal. After creating five of the best years ever of my teaching career, I felt a new call on my life. This time God said, "Take this message to the teachers of the world. Help them all to learn as you have to teach with authenticity, joy, and success." This is my life's work now.

That, my friend, is my story. I am delighted that it brought me to this moment shared with you. I discovered the ingredients of being a great teacher. This book is your opportunity to learn about them. Now that you know authenticity, joy, and success can be yours, what will you do?

Introduction

Congratulations on choosing this book. Whether you realize it or not, you've taken a powerful first step along a journey that will change your life. Let that sink in for a moment. Truly, reading this book is one of many small steps that will enhance not only your teaching, but also your life and relationships.

This isn't a book of quick tricks. If you are looking for a Band-Aid to fix up what ails ya, you've sadly chosen the wrong book. If you are looking for ways to reconnect with the teacher you dreamed of being, if you want to be a happier teacher than you are right now, if you want to teach with confidence in your own professional practice, if you want to have joy, and if you want to be a better teacher—in fact, a *great* teacher—then this is the book for you. Through this book you are going to take a journey that will guide you in reconnecting with your vision, mission, and passion, the picture you had of yourself when you were first called to teach.

We will begin by dispelling the myth of success that comes with believing you are what I call a "candle teacher." Our current paradigm supports an unrealistic and unhealthy result of being a teacher. I will expose this to you in detail. In chapter two I reveal the new paradigm for teaching, taking you on a journey through the five senses. In chapter three, I will define the great fountain teacher. Be careful as you read this part of the book. It will blow your mind, but I guarantee you'll be shaking your head and saying, "Yes, ma'am" even if you're not a southern gal like me. Once your understanding of this new paradigm is in place, I'll give you a brief overview of the nine steps in the paradigm shift in chapter four. Then we'll dig into the how-to section. In chapters five, six, and seven, we'll go deep into the nine-step process. I'll guide you through these powerful thought processes and life changes that will have you overflowing with passion and joy in your teaching, your life, and your relationships. Chapter eight will wrap up the process and lead us to the changes that happen as you shift your mind-set. I'll help you set up a support system for yourself, and I'll give you the opportunity to connect with others who are like you: passionate, committed, and ready to teach and live with peace and joy. In the final chapter, chapter nine, we'll clasp hands as longtime friends, understanding we are not ending, but beginning again, wiser, clearer, and more able than ever to embrace life on our terms.

Are you ready to begin? Great! Turn the page, and let's snuff out some candles.

Section 1

How wonderful it is that nobody need wait a single moment before starting to improve the world.

Anne Frank

One

Dispelling the Myth

A good teacher is like a candle; it consumes itself to light the path for others. Unknown

The "Good Teacher" Paradigm History

When you first read this statement, you may feel in tune with it. You may be saying to yourself, "Oh yes I am; I am this shining light, and I'm bright for others, and they will follow me." Sounds great, right? But take a moment to think about what it means. The model of a good teacher is one of a person who "extinguishes" herself in order to light the way for others. Oh my! Do you hear it? You're not good unless you totally burn yourself out for others. Yuck!

Go back a couple of centuries with me. In the 1800s teachers weren't allowed to marry, because this would take their attention away from their teaching responsibilities. In 1872, rules for teachers included items such as "after ten hours in school, the teachers may spend the remaining time reading the Bible or other good books." In the 1900s our candle teachers were told not to loiter at downtown ice cream stores, not to dye their hair, and certainly not to leave the city limits without the permission of the chairman of the board. The real kicker to these rules was this part: "Every teacher should lay aside from each day's pay

3

a goodly sum of his earnings for his benefit during his declining years so that he will not become a burden on society." Geez—not only must the teacher commit herself totally, but be sure not to burden anyone after you've burned out!

This dated paradigm of the good teacher "candle" is in direct opposition to what I believe to be a good teacher, or in fact, a great teacher. What would you rather hold as your vision: a good, burned-out candle or a great, overflowing fountain?

In the summer of 2012, I held a teacher retreat in Myrtle Beach, South Carolina, where we studied the Common Core State Standards for math and deeply investigated our beliefs about teaching. We worked to bring the two together. During the retreat we talked about this dated candle paradigm. When I first shared the quote with participants, they were agreeing, saying, "Oh yeah, that's great." Then I questioned them about its meaning. When we dissected it, the teachers in the room were shell-shocked. They didn't want to extinguish themselves in order to help their students. They were vibrant, wonderful, committed women, but they had families, pets, parents, and others who they wanted to live for. As committed as they were to teaching and their students, they wanted to live! Because you are reading this book, I know you are the same: committed to being a great teacher and having a full life.

As if extinguishing yourself for the sake of the classroom isn't bad enough, let me help you understand the other detriments of this paradigm. First, however, we must understand what we are up against. This candle paradigm has been around for centuries. Its principles are ingrained in you and in the people surrounding you. Therefore, if you are going to successfully shift, you need to understand fully what you are walking away from before we walk you toward the fountain.

Here's Why You Must Let Go of the Candle Paradigm and Its Principles

First, a candle needs to be lit from the top down. Right here I begin to disagree with the candle paradigm. I don't think that teachers need to be lit from the top. Yet, this is the reality. Mandates come down. Administrators tell (light) us (candles) what to do. They just strike the match and expect us to burn with it. Do you feel that? If so, does that feeling come to you from a place of joy or from a place of fear? I bet it is from a place of fear. Observations, write-ups, and threats of notes in your file have struck this fear in your soul.

Have you said (or heard other teachers) say, "Just tell me what you want me to do." This is a signal that frustration has brought you to the point of relenting to being lit. This is candle mentality. I shared it at one time. I've worked in schools where fear and mandates created the accepted culture. In my travels throughout America, I've also met many teachers who hold that type of fear, but that's because they've been conditioned to think that people at the top know best. Remember, the idea of lighting the candle from the top has been around for centuries.

If you are in the position where you're waiting for someone to tell you how to teach math, you're waiting for someone to tell you how to teach reading, you're waiting for someone else to tell you how to reach your struggling learners, you are in for a new way of thinking. This "light me up" philosophy is out. A new day is here. Doesn't that feel great?

Perhaps you're not waiting on others to tell you how to teach. Maybe you are certain that you know the right ways to perform your duties, but top-down mandates keep interfering with your practices. You are struggling against the fire attempting to light you. You too can celebrate; the new day is here. The fountain paradigm is for you too.

Before we blow out our candle paradigms forever, I want you to see the rest of its negative issues. This will strengthen your resolve to avoid defaulting back to the candle mentality when your fearful thoughts rear their ugly heads and try to dissuade you from being the fountain.

What Else Is Wrong?

What happens to a lit candle when a strong wind blows? Boom! Out goes the light. Strong winds could appear as a new principal, a special-needs child, a change in the schedule, a loss of planning time, or any other manner of disruption. When unexpected changes occur, the candle teacher goes out. She does not possess confidence in herself and her professional practice to continue brightly. She is snuffed. She waits to be lit again.

In contrast, here's a glimpse of the great fountain teacher. She studies, adapts and takes control and personal responsibility for continued growth and progress. The fountain teacher will continue to flow abundantly while the candle teacher will go out.

"If You Stand for Nothing, You'll Fall for Everything"

I think about this saying when I witness candle teachers being blown out by the winds of change. They do not have a professional footing on which to stand. Fear of "doing it wrong" has taken their confidence. They do not know what they stand for; therefore, they are blown out by mild winds as well as strong ones.

After a candle teacher is blown out, she will be lit again. The cycle will repeat itself over and over. This teacher will find relief in the next top-down mandate that arrives because she does not have a solid footing of her own beliefs and experiences to stand upon. She may hate the new mandate, but she'll be glad for it, because it will return her to structure and give her something to work toward, whether she believes in it or not.

Standardized testing in America is a great example of this relighting. When I first started teaching, we had district standards that students needed to master for the big test. The teachers in my district were lit. Within a few years, the state moved in and said, "These are the new standards you will teach." Essentially, the candles were blown out and lit again by the state. Now Common Core State Standards have surfaced. Candle teachers have again been blown out and lit again, this time by national standards. This is only one example.

Consider each time a new curriculum is adopted within a school. Teachers throw out the old and unpack the new. The cycle repeats.

Within both examples, teaching practices are altered to satisfy new requirements. Teachers' flames are blown out by fears of being unsuccessful if they don't teach for test results or according to the script of the new curriculum. This is a fear-based model of teaching, and it's due to teachers' lack of clarity about their teaching beliefs. Let's change this for you. Let's blow your candle out for good and get you started on the path to building your fountain.

Perhaps a Moment of Levity Is Needed

As I wrote the previous example, I was feeling a bit burned navigating those strong winds, but there are two more parts of the candle paradigm we have to debunk. Thankfully, this piece comes from a moment of levity.

The candle paradigm says that the teacher "extinguishes herself to light the path for others." If you don't get too caught up in the thought, this is hysterical. Let me explain. During my teacher retreat in 2012, one of the teachers in attendance pointed out to the rest of us that she did not want to enter her retirement "extinguished." She wanted to retire full of life and energy. To see and hear how vehemently she wanted to have a joyous life after teaching was invigorating. Hearing her debunk this portion of the candle paradigm with such dynamism was downright entertaining. She was right on!

Sadly, candle teachers do not reach retirement in this state. A journey of fear and dependence on others does not lead to a destiny of joy. Where you trod daily is the path that leads to the same end.

A state of fear, frustration, and burnout is not the model for us. I don't believe good teachers are people who burn themselves out. Additionally, whether you're coming to retirement soon or not doesn't matter; every year you have summer. You should not begin your summers burned out because you've illuminated the path for others during the school year. Surely that is not your desire. If it were, you would not be reading this book.

The Remaining Blob of Wax

Finally, what happens when a repetitively relighted candle burns to the end? What does it leave behind? Smoke and a wax blob. I don't want to burn out, stink like smoke, and become a blob. I don't believe you want to, either. Yet, this has been the pervading paradigm for a long time. Candle mentality has contributed to the stories we tell ourselves: "Oh my God, I've got to stay here seventy hours. There's so much to do. I've got to work myself to death. I'm going to be exhausted, but I'll come back in and do it again tomorrow anyway." I remember telling myself those stories and believing they were true. Consider these questions: Is that your authentic self talking? Is running around exhausted joyful for you? Is that the model of success you want to pass on to your children?

Enough Is Enough

Who wants to be a candle? Not me.
I do not want to be lit from the top down.
I will empower myself.
I do not want to be blown out with the winds of change.
I will develop confidence in my professional practice.
I do not want to rob myself and my family of my life because I teach.
I will be a joyful family member.
I do not want to end as a wax blob!
I will live with vitality.
Yippee! Out with the candle and in with the fountain.

Two

Behold the Fountain

A New Paradigm

*G*ood isn't good enough. You were called to be great. Today you will take your first steps on the journey of becoming a great teacher. Your journey begins by forming a solid foundation of understanding of the new paradigm. Here is the "great teacher" fountain paradigm; our new mantra. Behold.

A great teacher is like a fountain; she draws from the still, deep waters of personal growth and professional knowledge to serve others from her abundant overflow.

Wynn Godbold

Doesn't that sound a heck of a lot better than burning yourself down to a blob of smoke and wax? I am confident you're saying a big old "hell yeah."

The Fountain Picture

Sharing the fountain paradigm is exciting for me. This is my work-life mission: to change the paradigm so that *you* are inspired and empowered to teach with authenticity, joy, and success. No more burnout.

Let's consider the fountain. Picture in your mind a fountain that rises in the center of a pond surrounded by the pink, white, and green colors of spring. Imagine: you are the fountain. Hold this vision as I describe to you what you are doing.

Fountains draw into themselves water from the deep reserves of the pond. The water in the pond that surrounds you is the water of personal growth and professional knowledge. You, teacher, inherently love to learn. You love to learn your content. You love to learn best teaching practices. But you must also love learning about yourself. Personal growth and professional knowledge go hand in hand, because your authentic self is needed in the classroom just as much as your skilled self. This is why the pond that surrounds you, the fountain, is filled with both types of water. If you truly desire to teach with joy and success instead of being overwhelmed and burned out, you must ensure your personal growth works congruently with your professional knowledge.

I have always loved to learn. Before I became a teacher, I sold large group outings for the Myrtle Beach Pavilion Amusement Park. During my time at the Pavilion, I would receive tons of flyers and brochures in the mail about continuing education courses and seminars for sales people. These seminars dealt with topics such as time management, customer service, overcoming sales objectives; a plethora of seminars were being offered constantly. After receiving a few of these brochures I ventured into my boss's office and asked if I could attend one of the seminars. He liked the idea so I went to one, then another, and another. No one was paying attention to how often I was going so I just kept going and going.

That's when it hit me. I love to learn. Some of the seminars I attended didn't focus on topics that I particularly cared much about, but I went anyway. I couldn't get enough of learning. This experience was one of the pivotal events in my life that caused me to leave sales forever. With absolutely no plan in place, I left the Pavilion and began my quest to become a teacher. Deep in my soul, I knew being in an environment where learning was the goal was where I needed to be. Another important idea I learned during that time of attending so many seminars is to be great in any profession means learning more than just your craft. Learning about you and being in a state of constant improvement is critical to a lifetime of joy and success for all folks.

As a fountain teacher, you pull from the still, deep waters of what you know and continue to learn, both personally and professionally, to serve from your overflow. In contrast to the candle, you no longer wait to be told what to do, or be lit from the top. You know how to teach. You know what children need and the methods needed to reach your students. You know the groups to pull. You instruct your students based on your experiences and your continued study of your craft. You do not work in defiance of the mandates; in contrast, you know how to use them to teach congruently with your beliefs and support your students.

You serve authentically because you can. As others are waiting for the match to be struck and the light to come, you are already working, reaching, impacting, and influencing the lives of your students in powerful ways. You can do this because a fountain teacher knows what she believes; she acknowledges her experience and finds resources that support her. The fountain teacher does not wait for professional development to come to her. She seeks growth on her own. She is in command of her life, personally and professionally.

The Pond Is Constantly Being Replenished so that Its Waters Can Be Shared with Others

I had a conversation once with a dear friend and teacher colleague in which she said to me, "You know, all this 'stuff' is mandated to us, but nobody is hearing us. I've been teaching over twenty years. I've been watching kids learn. I've been helping strugglers to overcome. I know some things about kids and the way they learn. Yet no one listens to what I have to say."

She was right. Every one of us, whether you've been in the classroom for one year, six months, or fifty years, is a student of students. In the world of science, you would be referred to as a researcher. Consider it: if you've been planning lessons with an end in mind, predicting what might happen, preparing for the possible outcomes, teaching the lesson, observing what you see, monitoring and adjusting as you work, assessing the outcomes, and revamping the lesson to achieve different outcomes, are you not a research scientist?

You add professional knowledge to your pond every day. You experiment, you succeed, you fail, and you learn as you go by being in a classroom with live children. There is not a substitute for the kind and depth of information about children you gain year after year. Have you stopped to consider how much professional experience you bring to your craft? Do you have confidence in what you have learned over the years?

Don't underestimate the knowledge that you have of educating children. Too many teachers are buying into this wave of thinking that says, "We (outside sources, government types...) know better than you." Not fountain teachers. Fountains draw from the waters around them and know how to filter out the junk that falls into their ponds from the environment.

You, dear fountain teacher, must build and use an effective filter. If you don't already have a filter, relax. I'm going to give you the steps to build one in great detail in chapter six. For now, look at this overview and trust that I know how to help you. The first step of building your filter is to recognize your expertise. Know that you have valuable experience from the field. Commit yourself to building confidence in your professional practice through personal study so that you can develop a working filter that empowers your overflow of service.

In addition to filtering your waters, you also need to be able to communicate your professional beliefs and practices effectively. I have come in contact with too many teachers that cannot communicate their beliefs around teaching. They cannot express what they do, why they do it, or how it works in a manner that others understand. If we desire support for the job we do, we must learn how to communicate our findings in ways others can understand. Fountain teachers draw from the knowledge base they build in their ponds, and they learn how to communicate their practice so that others can understand and desire to listen.

Because fountain teachers have a depth of knowledge from which to draw, they do not operate in fear like the candle teacher who relies on someone else to light her. The candle teacher does not have the confidence to light herself, or she has been snuffed so often that she fears self-starting. Fear of "doing it wrong" stifles the candle teacher. Her confidence is gone. Somewhere along the way she bought into the myth that her daily work with children did not qualify her to continue successfully in her craft. Do you remember this statement from chapter one? "Just tell me what you want me to do." This statement is a sign of the fearful candle waiting to be lit.

As fountains, you are not fearful. You empower yourself to confidence by taking responsibility for your personal growth and professional knowledge. You are solid in your beliefs and practices. You monitor the growth in your students and acknowledge the ups and downs truthfully. You are empowered by, not fearful of, data. You are able to use it to improve your practice, and you can communicate your findings with ease. Your data/information about your students is not singly reflected through test scores; you examine the growth you see in the whole child. You, fountain teacher, believe monitoring, collecting, and assessing data is a good practice when done with the right mind-set.

Another benefit of the fountain teacher's confidence is that you are no longer in competition with your colleagues. You are able to ask for help when you need it. Your authenticity supports you. Fear of being in a professional learning community does not exist for you. Fountain teachers are not scared of being bested by the teacher next door, nor are they lit by the excitement of defeating the teacher next door. Fountain teachers delight in sharing from their overflow. Taking personal responsibility and being professionally grounded enables you to do this. Being an active member of a professional learning community is good for the fountain teacher. Your waters are to be shared, not hoarded.

You have the basics now. You understand the pond in which the fountain thrives. You see this new paradigm will empower you as you take responsibility for yourself. You understand the confidence you gain in knowing what you believe, being able to communicate it, and taking advantage of the opportunities to share. It is time to turn our attention more intently to the fountain.

Understanding the Fountain

Have you ever noticed how people love to gather at fountains? They are drawn in by the sights and sounds of the water. Often you can smell the freshness of the water as it shoots into the air and falls back to the pond. You can feel the refreshing spray on your face and perhaps even taste a droplet on your lips. Fountains are, in a word, magical. They draw us in with a magnificent five-sense experience. As you develop into a fountain teacher, people will be drawn to your magnificence too.

Let's examine the fountain using a five-sense approach. Continue your visualization with me.

Sight

Imagine coming within sight of a fountain perched in the center of a lake surrounded by the colors of spring. Look at the fountain. The sparkle of its water in the sunlight is dazzling. The movement of the water captivates you. The continuous flow mesmerizes you. It produces a visual kaleidoscope for your enjoyment.

You dream as you watch the water dance. You are free to stare and wonder. What if? Why not? Endless possibilities dance in your mind as a match to the unpredictable dance of the water that shoots from the fountain. You throw a penny in the fountain and make your wish, because you believe the fountain has the power to make your wish and dreams come true.

All that you see and believe about this fountain is true about you to your students, their parents, administrators, colleagues, and community members. They are drawn to you, the fountain teacher, on sight. The sparkle in your eyes when you talk to your students is as dazzling as the fountain water in the sunlight. The joy that radiates from you when you speak of your craft captivates your audience. The confidence you communicate when explaining the flow of your practice is mesmerizing. You are a source of joy for those around you.

You are a special representation of possibilities to parents. They send their children to you and make the wish that their dreams for their children will come true in your classroom. They believe you have the power to make their wish and dreams come true.

These are the sights we see when we look at you, the fountain teacher, empowered by the responsibility you have taken for your personal growth and professional knowledge.

Sound

Listen carefully. Can you hear the splash of the water? Do you hear a trickle? The sound of the fountain is soothing to the soul. Hearing the water move enables you to relax and enjoy the rhythm of nature. There is peace in moving water.

Often you can hear a fountain before it comes into view. Your curiosity is piqued because of what you hear. This draws you in for a closer experience.

Recognize that moving water also generates energy. It keeps algae from taking over the top of the water.

The sound of a great fountain teacher is similar to the sound of the moving fountain waters. Great teachers are soothing to listen to. They speak to children and adults in tones that are reassuring. Yelling and bitterness are not heard from fountain teachers. They employ better communication skills. Often the sound of a fountain teacher will draw others in for a closer look. They will hear what the teacher has to say and will want to know more.

Fountain teachers also recognize the rhythms of nature and are not thrown off balance by a change in cadence.

As a fountain teacher, you generate positive energy and engagement from others through the words you speak. You keep negativity from poisoning your classroom and your life.

Smell

Can you tell when rain is in the air by the smell of the atmosphere? Do you know the smell of fresh water? Yes, the scent of a fountain is fresh, clean, and easy to breathe. The fountain waters produce a natural smell. Imagine that you are standing before our lovely fountain. Take a deep breath. Inhale the aroma of fresh water moving in the air. Breathe in and exhale. The air is refreshing. It fills your lungs and enables you to release stress and tension as you exhale. You can open yourself to possibilities now that your stress has been relieved and your breath comes freely.

Think about positioning yourself as the fountain teacher. Can others tell you are a fountain teacher when they walk into your room? Yes, even by the smell. I'm not talking about deodorant (although, I would suggest that deodorant is a staple in the life of a fountain teacher.) Let's think more about your classroom. Take a deep breath. Is the air fresh? Is the smell free of dust, musty papers, old books, used carpets, and so on? Does the room smell clean? Is it easy to breathe in your classroom? Remember, "easy to breathe" for some folks means the air is void of artificial fresheners. Natural freshness is the key to making this sense come alive. Areas that smell fresh are clean. They are clutter-free. Carpets on the floor and displays on bulletin boards are free of dust and dirt. Items around the room are new and cared for. Old junk is not allowed to fill the space. (This includes any papers that were run off with purple ink! They do not belong in your fresh classroom.) Air circulates freely. People who enter this room are able to inhale deeply.

Additionally, the smell of freshness permeates what you do. You bring fresh perspectives to your lessons. You stay on the cutting edge of new ideas but also study time-tested practices for yourself before throwing out the old in lieu of the new. Even if you decide to keep the old, you will bring your fresh perspective and new vision to the ideas.

You have the gift to make hundred-year-old practices seem fresh and new.

When students are in your presence, they inhale deeply because you are fresh and easy to learn from. You enable them to exhale and release their stress and tension. They can open themselves to possibilities now that their stress has been relieved and their breath comes freely. You are the reason for this.

Touch

When you approach a fountain, you can feel the cool mist in the air. As the water shoots up from the pond, it is carried by the wind to rest gently on your face, hands, or feet. You feel the soothing sensation of the cool droplets against your exposed skin. Splashing and playing in the abundant flow of the fountain is refreshing. Your body is awakened by the tingle you feel.

So it is for others when they come in contact with you, the fountain teacher. Students especially can feel the gentle effects of your practice rest on them. They know that they can expose their fears and doubts to you because you will softly rest wisdom and knowledge upon them. You will not overwhelm, ridicule, or embarrass them for their shortcomings. You will soothe their fears. For these reasons, they delight in spending time with you. They want to splash around in the lessons you teach. Learning from your abundant flow of knowledge feels like play and discovery. Their minds tingle as they learn deeply.

Taste

You come to the fountain for refreshment. Nothing is more pure than the taste of the water from the fountain. The first cool sip that pierces the dryness of your mouth on a hot day is welcomed relief. Aah—imagine the lusciousness of the water as it wets your mouth. The taste of the water soothes and nourishes your body and soul, but a mere sip will not do. You desire more.

This is the experience others have when they come in contact with you. You are a source of refreshment for students, parents, and colleagues. The words, encouragement, ideas, and knowledge you share are that first sip of fresh water after a difficult hot day. They cut right to the heart of the matter and inspire children, parents, and your colleagues to continue working, to dare greatly one more time. Getting a taste or sample of you makes them want more.

Embracing this Paradigm

Embrace and embody the paradigm of the great fountain teacher through the five senses. Stop here and visualize yourself as this teacher. What do you see, hear, smell, feel, and taste in you that you can build upon?

We've investigated fountains and fountain teachers with all five of our senses. I hope that you are able to more fully appreciate the beauty of the new paradigm of what great teachers are. This is quite different than the old candle paradigm. The teachers I described flourish. They do not burn out. Even in the midst of storms and the changing seasons, fountains are able to serve from overflow and have beauty to offer.

The fountain, again, contrasts with the candle. We saw how easily candle teachers are extinguished with the blowing winds. Let's now look at what happens to our fountains when the storms hit.

Storms

Storms can take on many forms. Consider any top-down mandate. We know that candle teachers will be blown out by the strong winds that accompany these storms. Candle teachers will need to be relighted by forces outside of their own power. The same winds will blow against fountains, but the outcome will be quite different. When stormy winds blow against the fountain, the water from the fountain lands on the ground around the pond. When it falls onto the ground, it nourishes the grass. The overflow water of the fountain then reaches farther than

it initially had the opportunity to reach. The stormy winds of change actually serve to spread the impact and influence of the fountain teacher's water. Winds don't hurt the fountain—they provide the fountain opportunity to share outside of the pond.

However, sometimes the land around the pond is not grassy and able to receive the water as nourishment. Sometimes the land is plain dirt. Therefore, when the winds blow your fountain water onto these parts of the ground, the water mixes with dirt and mud is made. You cannot fight against this. Great teachers realize that it will happen on occasion. You will be ready for it and expect it. You will develop a plan ahead of time for dealing with the yuckiness of folks who are unable to embrace your new perspective. Whether those around you decide they like your influence or they do not, the winds of top-down mandates do not harm the fountain teacher.

A word of caution regarding your spreading influence is important here. When you get excited about becoming a fountain teacher and start working the nine steps outlined in this book, you will feel compelled to share your new outlook and way of life with others. Any time we make a positive change in our lives and start reaping benefits, we want to share. But let's remember actions speak louder than words. Most people don't like to be told about ways to change, because this implies they are not doing something correctly. Great fountain teachers do not desire to alienate others. In contrast, fountain teachers attract through their lives. You can share the changes you are experiencing within the nine steps when you are invited to do so. Your waters are then received by others as refreshing sprays. Fountain teachers do not pummel others with their water spray. We are fountains, not fire hoses. Keep the need for massive action and gentle sharing in mind.

Additionally, when you begin to change—especially when the change is from negative to positive—some folks will not like what happens within you. Your change will cause fear to creep into their psyches. This fear can cause friction between you and others. To put it a different way, "the shift will hit the fan." That is to be expected. This is one more reason we must act and wait for invitations to share, not pummel others with conversation. I will address the "shift hitting the fan" in chapter eight of this book.

You may even find that you experience a storm of conflicting feelings as you shift to intentionally living according to the nine principles in this book. Some days your soul will be as the grass receiving fresh water. You are nourished. Other days your soul will feel like the dry dirt around the pond—not ready to receive the benefits of water. You are caked in mud. This is to be expected. You are making a huge shift from candle to fountain. Assimilation of new information, ideas, and ways of life takes time, patience, and practice. It is a dance between your old self and your new self, cast with many subtle nuances. Be patient and stay the course.

After the Stormy Winds Come the Rains

We've addressed the winds of mandated change and the conflicting feelings you and others around you will experience. Now let's look at the rains of new initiatives. What happens when the rains fall? It doesn't take much rain to quickly snuff out a lit candle. We know our candle teachers will become extinguished in response to new initiatives. They will wait for professional development before jumping in. They will need to be told how to implement the new ideas (lit). What can we expect from our fountain teachers?

The rains of new initiatives don't snuff you, the fountain teacher, out; they actually fill your pond. They give you more water to pull from. The old water in your pond mixes with the new rains. As the fountain teacher, you will pull water from the mix of old and new, up from the depths and into your filter. After carefully filtering the water, you will project it to the world. The key to remember is that you will filter the water. You will make conscious decisions about what flows from you. You are an empowered teacher. You are an empowered person.

Make no mistake about it. The rains of new initiatives will always fall. But now you do—and you always will—have a choice in how you assimilate the rain waters. You choose what you pull up into yourself through your filter of beliefs and what you put back into the world through your overflow.

Let's talk in a deeper sense about these rains. Some of the water that you pull from your pond will resonate with your core beliefs immediately. You will readily pull them into your filter and will happily overflow them to others, but some of the water that lands in your pond will not be a match for you. In this case, you're going to let some of this water sit in the reservoir for a while. You need more time to look at it from many viewpoints. You may need time to research it for yourself. You may need to talk to colleagues about it. In other instances, you just need to sit on the new ideas for a while. They take time to absorb. Perhaps you want to test them against your own beliefs. You ask yourself, "Hmm, is that really something that I want to be spouting out to the world? Or do I need to work with that for a while?"

In another situation, you may want to allow some rainwater to rise to the surface of your pond because, honestly, it would be best if that new initiative just evaporated. We know that sometimes initiatives do that. They disappear. If you've been a teacher for any amount of time, you know sometimes initiatives rain down on us. Then the sun comes back up, and everybody starts thinking clearly again. If you can wait it out, some of those new-initiative rainwaters will evaporate.

I remember a time when portfolios became a big deal in my county. The plan was that every year we would collect work samples on every child in some sort of portfolio. This was a new initiative. The portfolios were going to be checked by administrators. If we didn't have one for every child some manner of trouble was going to rain down on us.

That idea lasted all of about three-fourths of one year. After three grading periods came and went without anyone asking to see my portfolios I quit keeping them. Apparently so did my colleagues. Portfolios were never mentioned again. You see portfolios in and of themselves are not bad. Some teachers use them with great success that truly impacts children's growth. The problem in my situation was that the portfolios were someone else's idea and it had no impact at the implementation level. This is why the practice simply evaporated.

In the case of these portfolios, I will tell you I was a bit of a candle. The eventual resolution to the portfolio mandate was an event that helped me see the beauty of being more like a fountain; another pivotal moment along my journey.

You see, candle teachers are snuffed out by these new-initiative rains. As fountain teachers, we let them fall into our pond and then we wait to see what happens when the sun shines. If they evaporate, we celebrate. If it's something we want to hold onto, then we assimilate the initiative, suck it up through our filter, and spout it out to the rest of the world.

Seasons

Now that you, the fountain, know that you can weather the storms with much more success than a candle teacher, you need to understand what happens in the seasons. You know it's nice to come to the fountain in the summer months. It's cool, refreshing, smells great, and feels good, but what happens when winter comes? And winter always comes. That's how the seasons work. It is the natural rhythm of the world.

The news is good. Have you seen ponds in the winter when the water freezes? If you're like me, a sweet southern sister, you've probably only seen this phenomenon in a picture. You know the one of the frozen pond with the water of the fountain also frozen in time, suspended in air. It appears as if the water is no longer moving. Everything freezes over. It happens. Winter comes.

In your life as a fountain teacher, the freeze can be due to professional responsibilities. I remember a time in my career when standardized tests became more important than children. Tests and performance were all we talked about. Ugh! I became so annoyed by standardized testing, my water slowed. My pond and fountain froze. I was distressed with my career choice, yet I believed, then and now, that I had been called to teach. I had known since I was in the third grade that I would be a teacher. Imagine my internal shame and anguish when I felt that I was failing at what I had been called by God to do. Perhaps you don't have to imagine. Perhaps you are grappling with this shame yourself, feeling as though you are failing at your life's mission. Your fountain is frozen.

Take Heart

After every winter there is a spring. Remember, this is the way of the world. Nothing lasts forever. Your spring will come. Before we celebrate spring, though, let me help you see the beauty of your winter.

Here you are. Your pond is frozen. Your fountain waters are suspended in time. You actually are still an amazing sight to behold. The white of the winter freeze holds a purity that is beautiful. As you find yourself frozen in professional dilemmas that feel so bad to you, recognize that you are pure to your beliefs. Yes, in the freeze, you remain pure. The freeze is part of the way you protect yourself. You freeze the flow in order to give yourself time to investigate, digest, and assimilate. You may even believe you are frozen beyond thaw but underneath the ice at the very bottommost depth of your pond, the water is still flowing. That's how it works. Down below what anyone can see, the water continues to churn. You are working to make sense of that which has frozen you. Fountain teachers have to stop the madness. You have to freeze things on the surface while you do the deeper work that distinguishes you from candle teachers.

And guess what? Even though you feel frozen and of no use, people are still drawn to you. People find you beautiful. Remember the purity we spoke of earlier? People will gather around you, even now. Some will even venture onto the ice of your pond. They will come to skate. They will enjoy your beauty and learn to navigate the world in a new way, with skates on their feet. They will play and laugh and create an elegant dance of new rhythms, all because you chose to embrace the winter. You continue to provide for others even when you feel frozen. Your deep freeze—your deep investigation, your commitment to honoring the depths of your passion—continues to provide for those around you. You are beautiful—*beautiful.*

Obstructions Can Plug Your Filter

You withstand storms and seasons. You acknowledge that professional obstacles will arise in your life, and you will deal with them with grace. But what happens when a personal obstruction happens? If you live long enough, you'll experience personal issues affecting your professional life. They could be wonderful or disastrous; for example, getting married or having a baby, a long-term illness or death of a loved one. Life happens, and it doesn't happen in a neat box away from your profession. You are a whole being. You don't live in compartments. Therefore, you must realize that your fountain filter will get obstructed by your life. Do not fight against your life. Embrace it.

I grew more as a teacher in the years surrounding my most traumatic personal time than at any other time in my life. We learn the most in discomfort. I never guessed I would learn so much about teaching while navigating the tumultuous waters of personal suffering; alas I did. I am convinced this is the way for many of us.

The year my mom had her stroke and subsequent Alzheimer's diagnosis I suffered a great personal obstruction to the flow of my fountain. I still did a good job as a teacher. I saw lots of growth in my kids, but I knew that because I was shouldering such an emotional load, my surface water really slowed. Interestingly, this year and the four that followed were years of deep personal and professional growth. It was as if the obstruction, much like the winter freeze, slowed me to the point of understanding myself, my passion, and my profession much more deeply. Slowing the surface flow allowed me to go to the deep water at the bottom of my pond. During this time I learned to relate to my students in new ways.

The pain of my mother's slipping memory caused me to look deeper in my students' eyes. When they cried about missing their mommies, I understood in a way I had never known possible. Alzheimer's was taking my mommy—I missed and wanted mine back too.

In the depth of my pond, I searched for and found a measure of water powerful enough that—when pushed through my filter—cleared the obstruction and increased my capacity to serve from a more abundant overflow. I had no idea prior to the storm of Alzheimer's just how authentic, open, and vulnerable I could be with students, nor did I realize the positive difference it would make in their lives.

The Essence

The storms, seasons, and obstructions always pass. Candle teachers go out repeatedly because of winds, rains, and snuffing caps. In contrast, beautiful fountain teachers are spread, nourished, and grow through the changes. We draw deeply and serve abundantly; every experience contributes in its unique way. This, my friends, is the essence of what it means to be the fountain teacher, and for me, this is what a great teacher is.

Three

UNDERSTANDING GREATNESS

When I let go of what I am, I become what I might be.

Lao Tzu

Defining a "Great Fountain Teacher"

*Y*ou've read the contrasting views between the old and new paradigms of what great teachers are. You understand the fountain paradigm. Now it is time for you to personalize this work. The next step on your journey toward being a great classroom teacher is to define the term "great teacher" for yourself. To go one step farther without beginning your vision would be like playing a game of sport with no goal. Imagine dribbling a basketball all over the court, looking up to shoot, and seeing there is no goal. What would you do?

The following exercise will help you build your vision. This is your exercise. Please, do not rush this process. To change your paradigm and create the ideal of who you want to be in your classroom, and in your life, you must first become clear about who that "great teacher" person is. How does she show up in the world each day? What does she value? What's at the top of her priority list? What keeps her up at night? Take some time to answer these questions openly and honestly. Be certain that you can articulate the answers to these questions and the ones on the following list. Write out your answers as you build a picture of this great teacher.

- What does the great teacher believe about children?
- How does a great teacher discipline students?
- What is the great teacher's role in the classroom?
- How does the great teacher act at faculty meetings?
- What does the great teacher believe about success?
- How does success show up in the lives of the great teacher's students?
- What kind of family and friends does a great teacher have?
- What does a great teacher do to take care of herself?
- What does a great teacher believe about her needs?
- What experiences have formed the great teacher's value system?

This is by no means an exhaustive list. It's merely an exercise to get you thinking about the concept of a great teacher. The answers to these questions must come from you. You cannot conform to the world's opinion and have an authentic, joyful, and successful teaching life. Take time to dig deep into your answers.

After you have completed this exercise for yourself, you may need a break. If you do, take one. There is not a rush to this journey. The journey is the fun part. The destination of authenticity, joy, and success cannot be reached if these traits are also not part of the daily journey. Travel at a speed that works for you.

⟶

Be aware, now that you have been digging deep into your belief system about what a great teacher is, you will likely have more ideas—some congruent and some challenging—pop into your mind throughout the next several days. You may catch yourself when you least expect it reflecting on this topic of being a great teacher. Loading and unloading the dishwasher, washing the car, or walking the dog may reveal an epiphany. Recognize it. Embrace it. I'm telling you, life is not going to continue in the same way as it has previous to reading this book. If you want to take a break and return; take your break. If you are ready to take another step, let's continue.

Our Definition of the Great Teacher

In this book, as within the organization I founded to support great teachers, the International Academy of Bee Sharp Teachers, I use three principles to frame my vision of the great teacher. These three principles are authenticity, joy, and success. I suspect that if you were to categorize your answers from the questions above, you could see that each attribute you assigned to your vision of the great teacher would fit within one of these guiding principles. For the sake of creating a common framework for us to work in, I'll share with you what I mean by authenticity, joy, and success.

Authenticity

The bottom line to authenticity is being able to be your true self in your classroom—openly learning with your students, connecting with them heart to heart, and acknowledging your gifts and your shortcomings—in short, being real with your students. I know that you've heard this before: "Nobody cares how much you know until they know how much you care." This goes double, triple, quadruple for teachers, especially for those of you who teach in geographic areas where the children come to school from unsavory environments. I'm talking about working with students who carry the mammoth-size suitcases full of the baggage of life to school with them daily. They're overwhelmed and come to school lugging all the junk with them. You, in particular, have to be your authentic self, your true self—the person who cares, the person who was called to teach—not somebody who is emotionally off-limits, hiding who you are from the children you teach.

Children with the most baggage are typically the ones who can readily smell a fake. I believe all children have a sense of this, but the ones who need you the most need *you*, the real you. Do not hide your authentic self from your students.

One caveat to this: if you are a miserable git; if you are angry at the whole world, then I'll tell you to fake it till you make it. If faking it isn't working for you and you authentically are angry and fed up with your daily living, I suggest you find a job that does not involve working with children. I don't want you to go into your classroom and be authentically angry at your life or your world and spew this all over your students. I do want you to be able to go in your classroom and be who you are, not pretending to be someone that you're not. I want you to bring your true self forward in your classroom, because if you're not teaching authentically, you will continue to feel depression, anger, frustration, a sense of being overwhelmed, and so on. You can't masquerade for forty-plus hours every week. I know that some of you are kicking up fifty, sixty, seventy hours at school. You cannot spend that much time on a consistent basis pretending to be somebody or something you aren't. It is exhausting and unsustainable. I'm here to help you be authentic in your classroom. This will bring joy and success. Life will be good again.

In chapter seven we will further uncover the steps to authenticity in the classroom. In case you have not noticed, by doing the discovery work of creating your vision of what a great teacher is, you've already begun to crack open your authenticity. You've come to grips with your belief system. The remaining work is about committing and living congruently with your beliefs. This is authenticity in action.

If you skipped the work of getting your clear vision, now is a great time to go back and grapple with those questions. Build your picture of the great teacher. If you want to revisit your description, you can do that now and at any time. Revising is the spice of life. As we grow, things change. Allow this to be fluid work. I know we teachers like to complete projects and check things off the list, but this work is the work of your life. Accept that it is ongoing. I promise acceptance of the ongoing will make it feel much better. Remember, you've begun a journey. You are not striving for the end.

Joy

The second principle I believe makes a great teacher is joy. Joy is an emotion that comes from deep within a person's soul. I do not define joy as a giddy, fleeting feeling. With joy, I acknowledge that sadness exists in life, darkness will sometimes shadow our lives, giddy happiness will come and go, and anger will surface and dissipate. But, unlike happiness, joy can exist in the midst of all the other emotions. It is a stream that flows within us always. At times it rushes rapidly, and we experience all manner of uplifting emotions. Similarly, at other times, it only trickles and is barely felt as opposing emotions are lying on the banks or providing dark cloud cover. The gift of joy is that no matter what the outside conditions, you can come to the stream of joy and find refreshment. It may be a small relief, but joy—the kind we, in the International Academy of Bee Sharp Teachers, want for you and use to define the great teacher—is persistent.

You might be giddy, angry, resentful, sad, disillusioned, happy, overwhelmed...a combination of many emotions. Whatever your state is, one of the goals of this book and the Academy is to get you started on your way to being a joyful person and a joyful teacher.

You must embrace one fact upfront: you cannot be joyful if you are pretending all the time. You must first get real with yourself (authenticity). You see now, building that picture of the great teacher is tightly connected to your joy. Being real is what allows you to have joy in and out of the classroom. Yes, we are focusing on being great teachers, but great teachers have great lives. This work is not compartmentalized to one aspect of your being. This work will touch you 360 degrees.

Success

The last principle I use to define a great teacher is success. Great teachers are successful in their own endeavors—that is, as they define greatness, so shall they be, and they set their students up for success. Great teachers know what they believe and teach according to their beliefs. They are also knowledgeable about the requirements of their profession. They are able to mesh the two success templates together and achieve. Great teachers enjoy their success and the successes of those around them. Great teachers do not fear losing the spotlight. They understand and embrace the thought of success abundance: there is plenty of success to go around. They help others achieve. Sharing is part of who they are.

My Wish for You

Now that you are familiar with the principles of my definition of a great teacher, I will share with you the desire I have for you. I want you to be your real self in and out of your classroom. Let's bring authenticity into your life. I want you to be joyful from the inside out—truly, deeply joyful, not just experiencing surface fleeting moments of happiness. I desire for you the life experience of real joy. Finally, I want you to be successful. I want you to recognize your success as you measure it against your deep beliefs about teaching, and I want you to be able to celebrate success for your students as you define it and as it is defined by society. I realize the bottom line of the world in which we live is test scores. I'm not ignoring that. I want you and your students to have that success, no matter how it is measured. Believe me, we either learn to play this testing game in a way that makes sense to us or go to Walmart and become greeters. I get that. Finally, I want you to find joy in the success of your colleagues. I want you to be part of a sharing society of teachers.

These three principles—authenticity, joy, and success—are the underpinnings of the remainder of this book. As I outline the nine steps to becoming a great fountain teacher, please keep these principles at the forefront of your mind. As we overview the steps, please keep in mind that this kind of work takes time to assimilate into our lives. It can turn your world upside down for a while, but it will straighten out, and things will start making sense.

I do not believe in overwhelming you. If at any time you feel the need to slow down your reading or to go back and reread parts, please take your time to do so. This is your journey. You are in control of your path. Read, reread, ponder, and assimilate at your pace. Here's a reminder of what's to come: the book is divided into three parts. Part one consists of chapters one through three, which you are now completing. Those chapters focused on building understanding of this beautiful new paradigm. The second part of the book, chapters four through seven, is devoted to sharing the details of the nine steps to becoming the fountain. You are beginning this section next. The final section of this book, chapters eight and nine, will help you deal with the changes that occur in your life as your shifts happen. I'll guide you through the negatives and give you insights that you can use to deal with the difficult times. Be aware: "the shift will hit the fan." I'm here for you when it does.

Section 2

Look within. Within is the fountain of good, and it will ever bubble up, if thou wilt ever dig.

Marcus Aurelius

Four

OVERVIEW: THE STONES USED TO BUILD YOUR PATH

We become what we think about.

Earl Nightingale

Three Bags with Three Stones Each

*e*ssentially there are nine steps in becoming a fountain teacher. To assist you in understanding the steps, I've broken them into three groups of three steps each. Imagine you hold three velvet bags ('cause velvet is so much richer than burlap). Embroidered on the outside of each bag is one word: Decide, Believe, and Share. Inside each of the three bags there are three beautiful, smooth stones. These are the stones you will use to build your path to becoming a great fountain teacher.

Decide

The first bag of stones you will reach into is labeled with the word *Decide*. Each of the stones inside this bag has a phrase etched into it. The first etching reads "Personal Responsibility." The second stone bears the mark "Professional Responsibility." The third stone has "Take Action" inscribed in it.

Making decisions based on these three principles is the first step of the process in becoming the fountain teacher. We will look at the three principles of decision more in depth in a few moments. Let's continue our overview of the bags and stones you hold.

Believe

The second velvet bag you hold is embroidered with the word *Believe*. Inside this bag reside three more stones. Etched in the first stone is the phrase, "Identify What I Believe is Right." The second stone is marked with "Identify What I Believe is Broken or Wrong." The remaining stone in your bag is labeled "I Believe I Can Do this Work."

When was the last time you examined your beliefs? It has probably been awhile. We're going to dig deep into them, because standing firm in your beliefs is much easier when you know them intimately and interact with them regularly.

Share

The final bag that holds your fountain stones is embellished with the word *Share*. In this bag you find the last three stones you will use to create your path to becoming the fountain. The first stone you pull from the bag has "Be the Change I Want to See in My Classroom" inscribed into it. Carved into the second stone is the phrase "Be the Change I Want to See in My School." The third stone says, "Be the Change I Want to See in the World." Fountain teachers show up differently than candle teachers. Fountain teachers are role models and are happy to share their lives by the way they live. You will discover your positive impact in your classroom, in your school, and in the world. I will help you find the joy in living and sharing your work with others.

In sum, these three velvet bags contain the nine stepping stones you will use to build your path to great fountain teaching. You have the overview; let's go deep now into each of these nine steps. You will begin by opening your velvet bag embroidered with the word Decide.

Five

Decide

The only person you are destined to become is the person you decide to be.

Ralph Waldo Emerson

The Nine-Step Process Begins: Introducing "Decide"

The first three steps of becoming a great fountain teacher involve conscious decisions made by you. Think about all the decisions you make on any given day. You decide to get up or remain in bed, to eat or to skip breakfast, to go to work or stay home. The list goes on and on. Now think about how many decisions you make consciously. Do you lie in bed each morning consciously thinking about getting up and consciously deciding to rise? Or, do you simply hit the alarm and get up? Have you ever arrived at work and wondered how the drive was? I know I've pulled into my school parking lot on a number of occasions and thought to myself, "Gee, how'd I get here so quickly?"

The reason we do things like this is because we live unconsciously. We have routines and patterns. We live according to preconceived notions; for example, I must go to work today. We are actually capable of living quite a bit of our lives unconsciously. There's really no reason to make those decisions daily. Or is there? What would life be like if we lived consciously?

As a fountain teacher, you will make decisions consciously. You will become empowered by the decisions you make. The days of living without choice, feeling stuck, and giving away your power are over. Living through conscious decision is empowering, but decision alone is not enough. There is a caveat that accompanies decision.

Consider this brain teaser. While out walking one afternoon you happen upon a lovely pond. In the center of the pond sits a lily pad. From the bank you can see there are three frogs seated on the lily pad. By a miracle of nature, you are tuned into frog-speak and suddenly can hear their conversation. You witness the frogs conversing.

Frog 1: I would like to swim. I will jump off this lily pad and enjoy the cool pond water.

Frog 2: Me too. I will enjoy the water with you.

Frog 3: Not me. I will stay here on the lily pad.

You heard the conviction of the frogs in their voices. Their decisions are firm. So let me ask you, how many frogs are left on the lily pad?

Is your answer one frog? If that is your answer, you are wrong. No, there is not a misprint in the book. Be sure you understand the question.

I'll recap: three frogs are sitting on the lily pad, and two of them decide to jump off. How many frogs are left on the lily pad? Did you read it correctly? If you did, you've likely come up with the answer: three. This is the correct answer. Why? Because decision requires action.

I can sit all day long and decide that I'm going to run a marathon. My decision is firm. I can decide the same thing today and tomorrow morning, just like those frogs decided they were going to jump off, but until they take the action, they are still seated on the lily pad. Until I get my buns up out of my chair and start training, I'm not getting any closer to running that marathon than when I made the decision.

Decision without action is nothing. You don't succeed by decision alone. Keep our frogs in mind as you investigate your first set of stones.

Stone One: Personal Responsibility

Could our frogs have jumped off the lily pad without first deciding to do so? No. Each action you take is a result of a decision; whether consciously or unconsciously, you decide. Some would say remaining on the lily pad was also a decision. Indeed it was. Consciously or unconsciously, you decide.

The point here is to make conscious decisions. This is how you gain power. Deciding from a place of strength and choice is the goal of the fountain teacher. Nothing starts. Purposeful actions can't be taken unless a conscious decision has been made first. To become a fountain teacher requires that you get active in your life. No more sleeping at the wheel. Deciding is big.

The first decision you make concerns personal responsibility. You have likely already made this decision. By choosing to read this book, you've said to yourself that you desire to be different than the candle teacher. The question is, did you make that decision knowingly? Are you aware that you want to be different, or did the title just intrigue you?

Your first stepping stone on the path to building yourself into a fountain teacher is to actually say to yourself, "Yes, I will be different. I will take personal responsibility." This decision might mean that you are going to be a different you than you used to be. By choosing to read this book, you've indicated you're looking to elevate yourself from being a candle to being a great fountain teacher. Is this because there's part of you that's teaching with a hole in your heart? You are missing something, and you know it. You are seeking. Be encouraged—whether this book fell off the shelf and hit you on the head or you found it on the Internet, you've opened it. You've decided! (And, don't look now, but you also took action! You've read to this point. You are actively pursuing your highest self.)

You're on your way. You've taken responsibility for where you are and for where you want to be. Celebrate. Seriously, get up and shake your bum! Then sit back down and read some more—but take a minute to smile at you. You've made a decision, and you've taken some action. These are the first things you do on your journey. There are many more decisions you will make along the way, but deciding to be different, to live actively, and to take responsibility for your actions sets the foundation for becoming a great fountain teacher.

Additionally, when you decide to be different, it often means being different than your colleagues. You are already aware that many of your colleagues are living unconsciously, just as you were. Some people will never step out of passive living. Your job is not to try and convince them. Your job is to love them and live according to your decision.

Simply realize this journey is different for each person. Some folks got burned and went out. Some folks are on the way to destroying themselves by burning their candles at both ends. You may be making a 180-degree shift. Someone else might only make a ten-degree shift. For others still, it's forty-five or ninety degrees. The one thing we know for all of us is that as soon as we extinguish that burning flame, healing can begin. The point is not to compare. Accept yourself. Embrace your journey. Know there is room in this great work for everyone and welcome your colleagues who will come in with you.

Your conscious decision making and taking responsibility for yourself began a small ripple that will change the world. Therefore, you must be truly—authentically—inspired and empowered. You may have been burned, but that became part of your past as soon as you decided to go for great.

Deciding to take personal responsibility involves opening up to a different way of doing things. You know the old saying: "If you keep doing what you've always done, you'll keep getting what you've always got." How do you know what to do differently? You begin by creating a vision of who, what, and how you want to be in the classroom, in your life, and in the world. That was very important. Did you catch it? You create (make active decisions about) who, what, and how you want to be (show up) in the classroom, in your life, and in the world. You need to understand this is not just waking, eating, driving, and working—rinsing and repeating. You are actively creating a vision of how you desire to authentically live.

You may say to yourself something that sounds like this:

"I want to be empowered. I want to go to school every day feeling good. I want to have a great attitude while I am there. I want to teach children in the way I think is correct."

Those are all conscious decisions that have to be made. Remember, showing up at school each day is not a conscious decision. Arriving at school and not remembering the drive is a sure sign of unconscious living. It totally lacks personal responsibility. If you have ideas about how you desire to show up in teaching, make your vision statement now. Actually write out the conscious vision of what you want to create as your school life.

If, however, you have been burning your candle self for so long you've turned to wax blocking the movement of your wheel of life, or you've anesthetized yourself by mentally checking out, the change you're making may require more effort. You may find it difficult to list the positive vision. That's OK. Here's some help. Know that you're going to dig deep during this exercise. Making the decision to do things differently than you've done before is where your transition and healing begins. You may not be able to even imagine what it was you wanted when you first started teaching.

If you are unable to tap into your desires to make your vision statement, try working backward. Make a list of what you *don't* want. Often when you're feeling burned out and are repeating a pattern of negativity, listing what you don't want can be easier than attempting to create a positive vision. I understand. Make this process work for you.

From that list, though, your work begins, not ends. After you list what you don't want, you have to flip each negative idea into a statement that expresses what you do desire.

Here are some examples of things you may not want:

- I don't want to go to school numb.
- I don't want to be snappy with my children.

- I don't really want to give that standardized test.
- I don't want to teach that.
- I don't want to talk to my students' parents in this way.

After you get the negatives out of your head and down on paper, then you flip the script. Ask yourself, one question at a time, "If I don't want this, then what do I want?" These are your personal responsibility decisions. "I don't want/ I do want": flipping the script helps us get the negatives out of the way and allows us to begin to travel the positive path.

For example, "I don't want to go to school numb" turns into "I want to go to school alive—in real connection with my students. I want to touch lives. I want to be positive." Do you see how one negative, when flipped, becomes a list of opportunities? Review your list of "don'ts" and flip them one by one. Then come back to this page. I'll be right here waiting for you.

I trust that you created your vision easily with a list or that you took the time to do the flip work. It is important not to skimp on these exercises. Your outcome is proportional to your input. This is your chance to really change your life. Do you need more time? Take it if you do. Otherwise, let's move on.

What Just Happened?

First, you made the decision to be different than the candle. Second and third, you decided what you do want and what you do not want in whatever order worked for you. There was a lot of personal decision making going on in that process. You became clear about your life. This is no small task. Take a minute to celebrate your thoughts. Celebrating life as you live each and every moment is a big part of living empowered. Fountain teachers are celebrators of life. Reflect once more on your personal decisions. Next, we will address the stone of professional responsibility.

As you started making personal decisions from your conscious rather than unconscious self, you began to change. These changes will now affect the kind of professional development you require. Your personal awakening will greatly influence your daily activity in the classroom. For example, let's say you identified collaboration among your students as part of your vision. Your statement might have sounded like this: "I want to look around my room and see teams of students working on projects individualized by groups." The conscious decision to incorporate this style of learning in your classroom creates a personal need for professional development. Your school or district may not be pushing this concept this year, or maybe you're piloting an idea. You can no longer wait, as a candle would, to be lit. Instead your personal decision now dictates your need to make professional development decisions for yourself. How juicy is that? Can you feel your empowerment? You are in charge!

In addition, now that you are awake at the wheel of your life, living from your empowered, aware self, you'll watch your kids and you'll think about things more deeply. You'll question events in your classroom and in your interactions, asking, "Why is that? How else can I break down that concept? Oh, she didn't get that today; I need to really think about my teaching for a few minutes; where can I go to find something that will help me reach that child?"

These are the questions of the empowered teacher. No longer will interactions appear meaningless. You will be tuned-in to the nuances of the children you teach. Between your personal-vision decisions and functioning from authentic awareness, you'll see your need for professional development change. It will take on new value.

Stone Two: Professional Responsibility

When you go to school powered by a clear vision and fully awake, your mind of teacher-learner begins to open up, and suddenly your professional development needs have changed. Now you have to make decisions about your professional responsibilities and the professional development you need. You say, "You know what, relying on someone else (the school/district/state) to provide me with opportunities to develop my professional practice is not good enough. My growth does not occur by being lit from the top down."

Waiting for and relying on others is out. Becoming alive in the way you teach and reach kids prompts you to search for your own ways to make a bigger difference. You begin to search, find, read, and talk about making classroom practices better. (Don't look now, but you're taking action on these decisions also.) You embrace the freedom to chart your own path to success. Imagine the joy you will experience by studying a practice that you believe in. When you become alive in your teaching, when you decide, "I'm great. I'm different. I am this fountain," you realize there is a wealth of opportunity to grow on your own. You look for the waters of professional knowledge to fill your pond. You are not overwhelmed by them. You call forth this information to fill your pond so that you can make conscious and clear decisions regarding your professional practice. After deciding to fill your pond on your own, rather than waiting for someone else to send the rains, you are then able to share from a beautifully overflowing fountain.

Let's put this into practice. At this moment, decide on and make a list of three to five things you will do to control your professional development. Decision and action work together. If you're struggling, here are some examples to get you started.

Try reading a professional development book such as *The Element* or *What Kindergarten Teachers Know*. Search online for books that support your ideas. You could also read articles in magazines like *Ed Leadership, Education Week,* or *Teaching Mathematics.* Many school libraries subscribe to teaching magazines, but they forget to tell their teachers about these resources. Ask at your school. You may be surprised by what great magazines are on the shelves. Dedicate time to searching TeachersPayTeachers.com, an open marketplace for original teaching resources, for purposeful classroom activities. Google articles on the Common Core State Standards. Join a national education organization. Fees are usually nominal, and the benefits abound. Membership into the organization I founded, the International Academy of Bee Sharp Teachers, is free, and you receive weekly professional development via short videos from me along with lots of other free resources. Visit www.BeeSharp.us to join.

Between the web, the library, and national and even international organizations, you will have all the professional development (PD) you can absorb. In fact, you'll have to decide carefully how to spend your precious and limited time. Fountain teachers know time is finite. They choose wisely where and how to invest it. Look for sources that give you your greatest return on investment. I challenge you to consciously investigate a PD source that you have never tried before. Make a decision about it. Is it a source you would spend your time with in the future? If so, decide how much time you want to invest. Decide how to fit that into your life. Decide where on your priority list this professional development resource fits. If you don't decide consciously how to integrate the new resource, it will most likely fall into the category of good intention rather than active learning on your part. Fountain teachers decide on the professional development they want, and they integrate it into their lives.

Even social media can provide you with opportunities to develop your professional practice. You literally have the world at your fingertips. But choose wisely! Be careful that you aren't engaging in negative discussions that go nowhere. There are plenty of those on the interwebs. Yuck. Don't fall victim to a circle of negativity filled with people who gripe and are not concerned with actually adding value to children's lives and the world at large. It's great if the group has opinionated discourse. It is wonderful to spend time in discussion with folks who have different views than your own. I advocate these interactions. Just make sure the group is positive. Consciously decide to spend your Internet time surrounded by positivity. Find a group where you can discuss differences in professional practice, where you can learn new ways of reaching children, where you can share your joys and sorrows, and where you can get and give good advice.

I know that teachers love Pinterest. I do too. There are tons of great ideas and classroom cuties out there pinned on folks' boards from around the world. Check it out. Grab what you can. Implement the ideas that serve you. I'm down with that.

However, here is a caveat. Be sure you are asking yourself, "What is the purpose? How does this meet my need? How does this enhance my teaching and make it the most effective?" Remember, great fountain teachers recognize that time is finite. When deciding on your own PD, ask the deeper questions. Go beyond cute to the opportunity for learning that is congruent with your beliefs about what children should know and be able to do. We'll visit your beliefs deeply in chapter six.

No matter the current trend, no matter the PD need, you are proactive. You've decided to take personal responsibility for your professional growth. Celebrate the step you just took. It is huge. You are in control. You are empowered by your decision making. Continue this practice throughout your career. Find articles, books, resources, and conduct your own research. Investigate the "next big thing" yourself, for now and forever.

Do you want to know what's even better than self-decided PD? Ooh—this is the part I love most about deciding to take responsibility professionally. The absolute best part is you begin to have faith in your own understanding and experience. Great fountain teachers trust themselves. Do you trust yourself? I work with teachers across America, and I hear them continually buying into the idea that they don't know what's best for the children in their classrooms. They make this candle statement: "Just tell me what to do." Have you thought or said that lately? No more. Now that you have taken responsibility for your own professional development, your level of trust in yourself is going to increase.

Get started by considering this: you're in a classroom with twenty-five (plus or minus a few) kids every day for 180 days a year. When you are consciously teaching, you are a living, breathing researcher of best practice. As a scientist of children's behaviors and learning styles, you watch them and study what works and what doesn't. You are building a great storehouse of knowledge. You are a conscious professional in charge of your life and teaching practices. As you take more responsibility for your professional growth and become more intentional about it, your faith in yourself and your practice will grow. Your faith in yourself will empower you to be the teacher you desire to be, the one in the vision you created in chapter five. Decision is the beginning.

Stone Three: Taking Action

Imagine pulling the third and final stone from your velvet bag labeled *Decide*. This stone is inscribed with the words "Take action." We have touched on this already to some degree, but let's make sure you understand the importance of this stone. Remember the frogs on the lily pad. Making the decision to jump in the water was not enough. There were three frogs on the lily pad, even after the decisions to jump were made. This was because the frogs did not take action.

Your life as a fountain teacher is similar to the life of the little frogs. Nothing happens for them or for you until action is taken. You've made your decisions. It is time to jump off the lily pad. Much of what we addressed in personal and professional responsibility was intertwined with taking action. You developed a vision of who you want to be in the world and how you want to show up at school. Creating your vision was an active process. If you have not created the vision, you should go back to chapter five now and do that.

⌣⟶

*Y*ou are actively building faith in your practice now by taking control and responsibility for your professional development. You are actively seeking and reading articles and books. You're looking beyond cute and questioning the activities you find online. Additionally, you are questioning the activities you've done for years just because you like them. Be honest: you have played Julie Andrews from *The Sound of*

Music at times, doing activities that are "A Few of My Favorite Things." But now you recognize that great fountain teachers move from "our favorite things" to practices that align deeply with our beliefs about teaching. You are now awake at the potter's wheel and are molding your students with purpose.

You are taking action. Congratulations. Again, celebrate yourself.

The Rub of Action Necessitates Boundaries

We cannot leave our discussion of action without first a word regarding boundaries. I know that some of you are big action-takers. You're ready to take on this new paradigm and rock the world. Caution: there's a rub to taking on too much. To be the fountain teacher, we are intentional about how we take our action. A huge part of intentional action-taking is setting boundaries. Too much action will rub you raw, wear you out, and essentially throw you into a state of being exhausted and overwhelmed; not very "fountain-ish," eh? This is why I brought up the idea that time is finite. I wanted you to see that fountains don't set unrealistic expectations. We are conscious and aware of what it takes to nourish ourselves.

Therefore, let's talk for a moment about setting action boundaries to support our flow. The first thing to understand about boundaries is that they are not constricting. You actually set boundaries in your life in order to protect the freedoms you cherish. Let's build your understanding through an example.

Let's pretend that you've set an intention to enjoy focused "home time" every night of the week. You've identified focused home time as a priority for you. It is part of what makes you energized for the next day and happy about teaching and life. Imagine this is part of the vision you created for yourself earlier in this chapter. One of the boundaries you might set to protect this intention is to stop reading school e-mails by nine o'clock. If you honor this boundary, you'll be able to enjoy focused home time. If you allow interruptions to this boundary, you will be self-sabotaging. Can you see how this boundary actually protects what you desire most? Note, this particular nine o'clock "cease and desist on e-mail" boundary is not meant to throw you into a frantic rush to accomplish all e-mail correspondence before nine. It is meant to protect what *you* identified as an important priority in your life: focused home time in the evenings.

Be careful right now. If you hear voices in your head saying, "That's terrible. I get my second wind at nine, after the kids are in bed. That's my quiet time to get work done," don't fret. That's an indicator that this particular intention doesn't resonate with you. It's not a signal that boundaries are awful. It's a signal that you are imposing my example as what you "should" want in your life. Stop right there: I do not advocate "shoulding" on yourself.

The key to living free through boundary setting is to start with intentions that are aligned with your priorities, what you desire in life. Then create the boundaries that protect your desires. Try this process with an intention that resonates with you. Name one thing you want in life or teaching. Then identify what it takes to make that happen. Finally, set a boundary to protect it. Writing out one vision statement and the accompanying boundary statement will help. If you skimped on writing it, pause now and write it out. This is your action step.

*D*id using your vision work better? Do you see now how your boundaries actually protect you? They free you to live and teach in the way you desire by keeping the interferences out.

Special Note that Comes with Your Clear Vision

When you examine your priorities, develop life and teaching intentions, and set boundaries to protect yourself, you need to keep this next idea in mind. It will make your decisions and actions flow with much less stress. Here it is: if you are 50 percent at school and 50 percent at home—mentally, you are 100 percent nowhere, because you are not 100 percent anywhere.

Take that in. Being physically at home but mentally at school (and vice versa) is essentially doing both half-assed. You are nowhere if you aren't 100 percent somewhere. When you embrace this mind-set, you will learn to turn your mind off of "home" and on to "school" when you walk into the school building. You will be able to give 100 percent of yourself to your students authentically. You will become tuned-in. Joy comes from this place of teaching 100 percent present in each moment.

The most wonderfully freeing piece of this total "present-ness" at school is that after being 100 percent tuned-in for the hours you are at school, you are then released to be 100 percent tuned-in to home. You discover there is no need for you to drag your big, fat schoolbag home with you. Your soul and your heart find freedom, delight, and peace in going home and being 100 percent at home after being 100 percent at school. No more robbing Peter to pay Paul.

Decide now to be 100 percent present wherever you are. Act on this decision by harnessing your mind into each moment. Protect your intention with supportive boundaries. You are on your way to greatness.

The Stones are Out of the Bag

Now you have awareness of the three stones that were held in the velvet bag labeled Decide. You have examined *personal responsibility*, the decisions you made to live consciously and the vision you created of yourself; *professional responsibility*, the decisions and action plan you made for taking charge of your own professional development; and *action*, giving movement to your decisions (the old git-r-done). Remember, without action, you'll sit on your lily pad forever.

You are also now aware of the importance and function of boundaries. Establish your boundaries around your priorities and embrace your newly protected freedoms.

Six

Believe

If you hear a voice within you say "you cannot paint," then by all means paint, and that voice will be silenced.

Vincent Van Gogh

The Nine-Step Process Continues: Introducing "Believe"

*D*o you believe in miracles? Do you believe the story told by the beggar on the street? Do you believe the sun will rise tomorrow? What do you believe? On this part of the journey, you will investigate your beliefs, discovering what you truly believe and what you've accepted based on someone else's belief system.

Look into the second velvet bag on display before you. The stones inside are inscribed with these ideas: *I know what I believe is right, I know what I believe is wrong or broken,* and *I believe I can do this work.*

The discussion surrounding your beliefs happens now, after you've built an understanding of the importance of making decisions and taking action. As you investigate your beliefs, you will go deep. You made the decision to take responsibility for yourself, personally and professionally. Now let's dig in and find out exactly what feeds your decision making.

Begin by asking yourself some questions:

- What do I believe is the role of the teacher?
- What is the role of education in the life of a child?
- What do I believe children need to learn?
- What do I believe children need in order to learn?
- What is the role of the school in regard to the basic needs of the child?
- Why do I exist in my classroom as a teacher?
- What am I really supposed to teach kids?
- What does my heart say about teaching?

These are tough questions. Give yourself time to think about them. When an answer pops into your head speedily, slow it down. Look at your answer and examine how it rests with you. Where did that belief come from? Who in your life influenced your thinking? What were the circumstances in your life that developed this belief? Does your belief come from a place of wholeness, love, and joy, or a place of fear, scarcity, and judgment? Knowing the basis of your beliefs is central to creating the life and career of the great fountain teacher. Recognize that your answers are not static. Your answers today may not be the same answers you come up with tomorrow. This sort of work is messy. It can feel confusing. When you dig around in your core values and belief systems, there is a lot of gray; you do not live in black-and-white. Learn to see the beauty in the varying shades of gray.

Your core belief work supports you in being a fountain teacher, because your beliefs are the filter through which you pull all the waters of your pond before taking them up into yourself and sharing them in your overflow. If you are unaware of what is important, even fundamental, to yourself, you will find yourself in teaching and living situations that constantly drain you of your life energy. When your belief filter is finely tuned, you are able to process the waters of the pond more effectively.

You are more able to keep out what is not a fit for you. You are able to see disagreements between your core values and the values held by the school in which you teach.

Let's look at an example to help us understand. Suppose you come to the core belief that discipline in the classroom is priority number one. You will do anything to keep those kids in line. You believe that getting in the face of a child and yelling at him or her is an acceptable way to keep order. Whether you agree with these beliefs or not doesn't matter for our example. (I don't agree, but for the example let's roll with it.) What matters here is that the person who holds these beliefs is aware of them. Why is this important?

Schools have cultures. They have norms. Knowing your beliefs opens the doors for you to choose the role you play at your school. Being aware brings choice and decision to you. If the person in our example is teaching in a school where yelling at students and getting in their faces is an unaccepted practice, then our example teacher does not fit in. He or she will be in a constant state of disconnect. The example teacher has a choice, just as we all do. He or she has to decide whether to assimilate to others' beliefs or to stand up for his or her own, yet contradictory, beliefs.

The example leaned toward the black and white—yell or don't yell; stay or leave. This is where those shades of gray come into play. Most examples aren't this cut-and-dried. Within any teaching situation you have to negotiate with yourself. When you are super clear about what you believe, these negotiations are much easier. You can decide to leave your current work situation to find a situation that more closely aligns with your philosophy. You can decide to stay in your situation, recognizing the differences, but being willing to play by the rules. You can decide to stay in your situation and fight for your beliefs. Any decision you make is fine, as long as you made it consciously from your empowered position. No victim mentality is allowed.

You have choices. You are in charge. You may have bought into the theory of "I'm not happy, but I can't afford to leave." Check into that statement. Know that you made a choice based on what you value most.

Why can't you afford to leave? Is it because you are afraid of moving from your hometown to find a school where you fit in? Are you scared you won't get hired anywhere else? What are the ties that are binding you to the present? Do you recognize that your decision to be in an unhappy situation is related to placing a higher value on ideas other than your happiness? In this example, the highest values were given to the fear of moving (otherwise stated as valuing staying put), and the fear of not being hired again (otherwise stated as valuing the belief that you are not good enough). Let that sink in. This is not the way of an empowered fountain teacher. Now digest this: where you are right now is a product of the decisions you've made thus far. Own them.

This is not condemnation. This is a realization of previous choices and the power you have over your future choices. Just writing that sentence made my heart skip a beat! The joy of creating the life you want is in your hands. Good gravy, that makes me excited for you.

Teaching as a fountain is empowered teaching. You are not a victim of the circumstances in which you teach. You don't see children as victims. You are not blind to obstacles, challenges, and hardships nor are you overwhelmed by them. You know what you believe. This knowledge equips you to tackle the tough issues. It enables you to reach your students authentically, with joy, and success.

Throughout this chapter, as you examine your beliefs in greater depth rest assured this book does not exist to judge your beliefs. It exists so that you will know and understand yourself in order that you can choose your roles in life.

Get to Know What You Believe

Start with the bulleted list of questions I shared at the beginning of this chapter. Get still and give yourself time to form the answers. Once you have answers, follow up with the deeper questions I asked in the paragraph following the list. The answers you form today may need to be revisited. Over time you will experience situations that will challenge your beliefs. You will process change. You will shift, alter, dismantle, and reconstruct your beliefs. This work is messy. It is the work of your lifetime. It is the work of the joyous soul; constantly learning, growing, expanding.

When you begin actively living and teaching according to your soul, your joy will overflow. You will spill out to your students, their parents, your colleagues, and your own family the joy of being authentically engaged in your life. Aah—this is part of the beauty of the fountain teacher.

If answering the questions from the bulleted list and the paragraph that followed was a great start for you, but you want even more or perhaps you got stuck in your attempt to answer those questions, read the next paragraph. If you got bogged down by that exercise, continue reading but commit to coming back to this work. Skipping the challenging work robs you of the best opportunities for growth. No wimping out! The next exercise is designed to take you further into knowing your beliefs.

You can use this exercise anytime you get stuck or want to go deep into your belief. The exercise is to simply ask yourself five "whys." For example, you say to yourself, "I think that we should not have standardized testing." Now ask yourself, "Why?" After you answer that "why" question, ask another "why" question based on the answer you just gave. Repeat this process until you have asked "why?" five times. At the end of five whys, you will typically arrive at the root of the belief. Work the questions now. See where they take you.

This process is not a quick fix, folks. There isn't a quick fix. If you were looking for a teaching tip that you could do in thirty seconds and be great, you won't find it here. You won't find that tip anywhere. It does not exist. Anything worth doing is worth doing well, and things that are done well take effort and time.

Do you love learning about yourself? I always have. This is fun work! Here are some additional questions to guide you deeper into your beliefs. Remember, you can use the practice of asking five whys at any time with any question, thought, or belief.

In what kind of space or environment do I believe children learn best?

What do I believe children at this age or grade need to learn?

What do I believe about the Common Core State Standards?

What practices do I believe are best?

What does an effective classroom look like? Sound like? Feel like?

At my teacher retreat in 2012, we did some of this work on our beliefs. In the beginning, the attending teachers said, "To be a great teacher means you love everybody, and that you're happy, and you know your content." Good start, but then I asked them to go deeper: Why does loving everyone matter? Why do you do that? What does "loving everybody" look like in your room? At this point, the teachers started getting down to their beliefs, bolstered by images they could see and hold on to. This was the point at which they began to develop an understanding of their individual belief systems. This was the start to empowerment, choice, authenticity, joy, and success, as they each defined it.

Take a moment to review your beliefs again. Do you have a clear vision and understanding of why you feel the way you do? Are you pleased with what you see? This is your exercise. Take time to enjoy the journey.

Let yourself be drawn by the stronger pull of that which you truly love.

Rumi

Believe: What I Believe Is Wrong or Not Working

Defining what you believe is right is stepping stone one. Now you have to identify what you believe is wrong. I've mentioned before that sometimes it is easier to say what is wrong than it is to articulate what you believe is right. I hear it all the time as I walk down the hallways in schools. I see pods of teachers congregating and saying, "This is not right for kids." When I ask what *is* right, often they can't articulate their beliefs. But they are super clear on what's wrong. So this next step will likely come much easier to you.

Take time now to list the things you believe are wrong or broken with education, your school, or the way you teach. You can probably list off the top of your head fifteen things right now. That's OK. In fact, it is actually a good thing. If you can bring the negatives into your awareness, then you have the opportunity to consciously deal with them. Notice I did not say you can wallow in misery and complaints. Opportunity exists when you have awareness. If you teach or live in a state of unknowing, then you have no options, no choice, no power. That is not you.

Identifying what goes against your belief system is the first step to dealing with these obstacles. No longer will you live like the ostrich with your head in the sand. You will take the second step, which is to deal with the obstacles you have identified. Some wrongs you identify will be within your power to change. Others will not. The ones you can change are the easy ones. They may take work, but you can fix them. The wrongs that are out of your control to change will require more effort on your part. Nonetheless, you have choice. With choice comes empowerment. Let's look at an example of how to be empowered when you can't change the situation. Then you can take additional time to make your "what's wrong" list and go deeper into understanding how to deal with it.

Here's an example for you. You may think standardized testing is wrong. You may also feel it is out of your power to change. What's a fountain teacher to do? Now that you've identified one of your core wrongs, you are set to deal with it. Use the process of asking five whys. "Why do I believe this is wrong?" Ask why for four more times. See what comes up. When you come to the core realization of why this is so wrong, you can begin to deal with it. Let's say, after asking yourself five whys, you see the bottom line is fear.

Go deeper. Examine that fear. What are you afraid of? How likely is it that your fear will come to fruition? What is a feeling you can concentrate on that is just a little bit better than that fear? How much of your fear is grounded in reality, and how much is invented?

At one time in my teaching career, I had a colleague who would come to team meetings quite stressed. She was constantly saying, "I don't want to lose my job if the district comes in and sees me doing ___." You can fill in the blank with any number of things. Finally, one day I asked her, "How many times a year does someone from the district come to your room?" Her answer was one, and they had already visited for that year.

She had created a huge perceived threat that was not grounded in reality. Consequently, she kept herself in a state of constant fear. She continues to teach as of this printing. I believe this would be her twenty-eighth year.

You may be thinking, "Yeah, but they are in my room constantly." Don't get hung up there. Look at the example for what it is. It is a way of showing you that we often place tremendous stress on ourselves that is not based in reality. Truth be told, she followed most of the rules. She was a successful teacher. Her students did well year after year. Sadly, she lost out on a lot of joy because she entertained with vigor her perceived reality, which was full of fear.

Ask yourself, "What do I believe is wrong?" But don't stop there. Get to the root of the problem using the five whys so that you can deal with the problem realistically. The issues you face are only as big as you allow them to be. Your perception of the wrong is your reality. Choose your perception wisely.

You may doubt that you can choose and create your reality. For that reason, let's look at another example. Let's say you work for a principal who values test scores above all else, and this doesn't match your belief in educating the whole child. You're thinking, "Well, dang it, I can't fire my principal, and he's the root of all evil at this school." What can you do? What are the ways in which you can feel a little bit better toward him? What is one small thing he does that opposes your view slightly less? When you find one small measure of hope, be grateful for it. Capitalize on it. You'll find that once you approach this problem with a little dose of gratitude, more opportunities for gratitude will arrive.

Although you cannot fire your principal, perhaps there are some small shifts you can help him or her make. Additionally, what are the things that you can change? You may find things in the school that you can positively impact. Likewise, you may find that the change in the situation will come 100 percent from you. Use this phrase as your new mantra: "I am willing to see things differently." It doesn't mean you'll change your thinking. No. It doesn't mean you'll give in. It simply means that you are willing to look at situations differently so that you can get new perspective, you can open new thought patterns, and you can see new and possibly more affable approaches for everyone. Different does not mean giving up or giving in. It means broadening you. Oooh, this is exciting stuff!

If you haven't already, take time now to list what you believe is wrong. Let it rip. Get it all out, then come back to deal with it by asking the five whys. Brainstorm first; ask the whys second. Revisit and apply your new mantra to the situation: "I am willing to see things differently." Then come back here, and we'll move forward.

⁓

*W*elcome back. You just did a load of deep work. Be sure you're ready for the next part. If you need a break, take it. Otherwise, let's move forward.

Think back to the first stone we placed on our path to being fountains. It was the stone of personal responsibility. This is a perfect opportunity for you to take responsibility for your feelings, your actions, and the way that you react to things. When we come face to face with things we do not agree with, we have choice.

Do you realize that the letters used to spell the word *react* are the same ones you use to spell the word *create*? It's only a matter of ordering the letters. This shows us we can *react* to what is thrown our way, or we can choose to *create* our overflow. You are in charge of everything having to do with you, whether reaction or creation. So, if you're mad about something, that's your decision. If you're glad about something, that is also your decision. These are examples of your reaction choices.

When you go deep into fountain teacher mode and take personal responsibility, you have an opportunity to create the situation. You find your power in the choices you make to influence circumstances. You choose your stance before the "something" comes your way.

The bottom line is you can't always change the things you don't like. But you can change your reaction or create a different way of looking at the situation. Your empowerment will be found in the place of creation and choice.

Let's go forward from the stone of knowing what you believe is wrong by invoking the Serenity Prayer:

God grant me the serenity to accept the things that I cannot change, courage to change the things I can, and the wisdom to know the difference.

Think about the wisdom in knowing the difference between what you can and cannot change. Accepting what you cannot change does not mean rolling over and taking it. It means acknowledging what cannot be changed and then creating your own plan to deal with it or walk away from it. It also includes changing the inside of you, which can be done at any time, because you are the one certain thing you have power to create. You are solely responsible for you and can choose.

You may be feeling a bit shaky in your ability to choose and create. You may be psyched about your newfound ability to create. You may be anywhere in between. Wherever you are is the perfect spot for you at this moment. Embrace yourself. Given the various levels of comfort you may be experiencing, I have purposefully designed the next stone in your velvet bag of Believe to speak right to your confidence. It is imperative you believe you can do this work.

Believe: I Can Do This Work

You have laid five stones in your path to becoming a great fountain teacher. These stones are:

1. Decide: personal responsibility
2. Decide: professional responsibility

3. Decide: taking action
4. Believe: what I believe is right
5. Believe: what I believe is wrong

The sixth stone you will lay in your path is the stone that says "I can do this work." Let me be clear. You must believe in yourself and your ability to teach from the authentic, joyful, and successful place of the fountain teacher. You cannot enter your classroom questioning whether or not you can do the work. You must have confidence in your ability. And you can. Here's why. Fountain teachers are able to believe in themselves, because they take responsibility for their personal and professional development. They are teachers of action. They develop and maintain healthy boundaries. Fountain teachers have clearly defined belief systems. They are confident in their practice because they know their hearts. They measure the next "new thing" against their beliefs. They filter the rains that pour into their ponds. Fountain teachers are in the practice of creating their realities. They minimize reactive living. These are the reasons you can do this. You are becoming the great fountain.

Believe in yourself. No one else in the world has had the same two weeks, two years, five years, ten years, or thirty-five years of teaching experience that you've had. No one else has been a student of your belief system. You have. You are the only one who is actively taking responsibility for you, personally and professionally. You are the one developing yourself, creating your conscious teaching practice, and willingly seeing obstacles from many perspectives. As you continue to be a student of your best practices, of what works in your classroom, and of the children you teach year after year, you are building a knowledge base that no one else has. Embrace your experiences and stand upon them as part of defining your professional savvy. Learn to articulate the knowledge you have accumulated in your years of practical study and on-the-job research. This will bolster your belief in your ability to do the work of the fountain teacher: the Great Teacher.

Grow confidence in your beliefs by reading, learning, and discussing ideas with others. Hear what's on their minds. Think about it. Ask yourself if something they said is worth a tweak to your beliefs. Seek out others who have taught for long periods of time. Find a book or a magazine that pushes your professional buttons. Share on Facebook and Twitter. Join some teacher groups and listen to what other people say. Put your beliefs out there also. Be challenged and be questioned. This will help solidify your beliefs. Do these activities from a place of love and willingness to learn, and you will become empowered in your truth. It's amazing what you can gain from sharing with and listening to others. Enjoy your freedom to change your mind or to stand firm.

Engaging in these types of activities will give you the confidence and ability to believe in your teaching practice and in yourself: the Great Teacher. Tough times and challenging requirements will come. Rains and debris that test your confidence in yourself will fall in your pond. But with your strong filter (belief system) in place, you, the fountain teacher, will know what to focus on and how to create a reality that supports you and your students. When the junk in your pond tries to get through your filter, you'll say, "Hold on a minute." Your belief filter will slow these challenges from taking over. You'll find and allow yourself time to deal with them. You'll look at them in more depth. You'll learn more. You'll ask questions of the people who are giving you that junk. You'll ask, "How do you know this? Where did you find this? What makes you feel we should believe in this?" Your filter system will cause you to be a challenge to the new ideas. Not from an ugly place, remember; it's from a place of love and willingness to learn, but, let's face it, some of the stuff that falls in your pond is going to be junk. You have to ask questions.

Be careful here. When you come across junk do not let it get caught in your filter and clog your progress. Fountains do not flow when their filters are clogged. Yet this is where scores of teachers get stuck. Clogs are what keep many from becoming overflowing fountains. Look at this example. A mandate comes down from above: "Keep track of X,Y,Z on this form for every child." You hear your colleagues, *"Ohhhhh,* I can't believe they've asked us to do another piece of paperwork. I've already got five pieces of paper on every child." Wah-wah-wah. On and on they go. Their negative energy of reaction runs rampant. They are not flowing. They are clogged. This is the time when a fountain teacher moves out of reaction and into creation.

Fountain teachers will create systems in their classrooms that help paperwork flow. They will monitor how much time meaningless work takes from their day and will make a logical case for getting rid of waste. They will seek to understand the purpose behind the task, knowing that a larger view often helps new tasks and requirements make more sense. In addition, the fountain teacher is aware that, given enough time, some things will simply evaporate out of her pond. After a mandate rains into the pond, the sun will come out and shine on the water. If you give it enough time, evaporation happens. This new paperwork mandate may very well fall by the wayside. If that happens, will it have been worth all the frustration and negative energy produced by the clogged teacher? How much time are they willing to waste in negativity? One minute is one minute too long.

Keep in mind that no matter what happens after the rains of "new and improved" fall into their ponds, fountain teachers always believe in their ability to do the deep work: teaching with authenticity, joy, and success.

Go forward in faith, dear teacher. If you need to, lean into my faith. I am holding space for you—space of deep belief in you.

Seven

SHARE

*Successful people are always looking for opportunities to help others.
Unsuccessful people are always asking, "What's in it for me?"*

Brian Tracy

The Nine-Step Process Continues: Introducing "Share"

Your last set of stones is contained in a third velvet bag. This bag is embroidered with the word *Share*. From this bag you pull the first stone, which instructs you to be the change you want to see in your classroom. The second stone says to be the change you want to see in your school. The third one tells you to be the change you want to see in the world.

What does "be the change" have to do with sharing?

Glad you asked. The work you are doing here, in deciding and believing, is soul work. It will fundamentally change who you are and how you show up in your classroom and the world. Rather than running around telling everyone how you've changed and how to be like you, I suggest that you share by "being the change."

"Your actions speak so loudly, I can't hear what you're saying."

This quote is truer in becoming a fountain teacher than in some other situations. You are looked to as a role model by students, parents, colleagues, administrators, and community members. Your actions will speak louder than empty words. If you live your fountain ways, people will take notice without you having to tell them about your joy. They will experience it. Showing your authenticity, joy, and success through your deeds will resonate with folks. Your overflow will create ripples in the pond surrounding you, the fountain. Start with those closest to you: your students.

Share: Be the Change You Want to See in Your Classroom

What changes have your crystal-clear beliefs brought to mind about your classroom? What is your vision of your classroom? How does your classroom look, feel, and sound? When you place your beliefs about learning beside what is happening in your classroom, do you see any inconsistencies? I want to help you deal with these. This is where sharing by being the change begins. Let's look at an example.

Suppose you identified active listening as one of the fundamental steps to learning in the classroom. Yet, on a daily basis, you don't feel your students are listening as attentively as they need to in order to learn. Let's check in to see if you can share your active listening belief by being the change. In regular teacher-talk, this means modeling. You must be the model of what you want to see. Remember, your actions speak so loudly your students can't hear what you're saying. Be the listening change.

Look closely and answer honestly. Do you give your students your 100 percent attention? Or do you multitask? Do you say to your student who is talking to you, "Yeah, go ahead, uh-huh" as you are shuffling your papers? Be honest with yourself. A realization here may hurt a little, but often teachers I work with will stop here and tell me, "Oh my gosh, I stand and I teach in front of my room, and I expect everybody to be all eyes on me—eyes, ears, and hearts. You know, active listening. Give it to me. Pay attention, Johnny. Look over here." But when it is Johnny's turn to speak, they realize they are not looking at him.

Are you intentional and in the moment with your students? Have you made the decision to be that kind of teacher? Are you listening to each one of your children in the same way you desire that they listen to you? Think about it. This is only one example of bazillions where you can share your fountain ways by being the change you want to see in your classroom. Share through your actions.

Here's another example to consider. Do you participate with your kids when they go to field day, to a play, to an assembly, or to the computer lab? Are you in it with them, or do you observe as a bystander? I know that some of you are saying, "Well, I've got to have a moment of down time, and the computer lab is the only time I get my down time." I get that. It's OK as long as you've made a conscious decision about it. If you are allowing yourself this time out, by decision and by intention, that's one thing. If you are unconsciously timing out, that's a whole other story and not in alignment with great teaching.

Modeling behaviors for your students is so important. Hopefully for you, the examples above are enough to shine a light on the importance and subtleties of what being the change you want to see in your classroom means. However, if you are not yet a believer, take in this experience I had while working with one teacher in the United States. Honestly, this happened.

As part of the work I do in schools, I often visit classrooms, observe teachers, and then debrief. On this particular day, I observed a teacher attempting to instruct his class. I say attempting, because the class was in chaos. For those of you who have spent your careers in peaceful schools filled with fairly well-mannered, average and above-average achieving students, this example may be hard to even imagine, but I tell you, this is one of the times you need to employ your new mantra: "I'm willing to see things differently." You will have to trust my experience and see that things happen around our country differently than you perhaps have been acquainted with. Reading this example will probably open your eyes a bit to understanding the media and political outcry about our education system—the whole big one.

Here's what happened. I was observing a fifth-grade class. The students were out of their seats and talking over the teacher. It appeared everyone was using his or her voice to vie for the top spot in the room. The volume of noise in the room was nowhere near what I consider conducive to learning. I was seated in the back of the room. My purpose there was to observe math instruction, a difficult task in the chaos. The teacher was attempting to conduct a lesson. He called some children down, reprimanded others, and introduced the topic amid the noise. But here's the specific event that makes our example of sharing by being the change you want to see in your classroom necessary. The teacher saw a broken pencil on the floor. He picked it up, threw it across the room, and into the garbage can. The pencil literally whizzed by the head of a child, who was, incidentally, out of his seat. The teacher was a part of the problem, not the solution.

If a core value of this teacher was to have learning take place in a safe environment within the classroom, the teacher was not acting congruently with the belief. To share this belief, he would have needed to model the safe procedure of how to throw away the pencil. (I am solely dealing with this specific event, although there are clearly many other issues at hand.)

There was no fountain teaching going on here. There was not a hint of being the change you want to see in the classroom. His decision to teach without joy was further supported during the debriefing session. The teacher made statements such as my kids are awful, they won't listen, and they can't be controlled.

There was neither professional—nor personal—responsibility being taken here. The teacher did not realize he was part of the problem. He modeled several behaviors repeatedly that he didn't want his students to emulate. Just in case you're missing it, I'll spell it out loud and clear:

Don't say that your kids are throwing stuff and you can't stop it when you modeled throwing a pencil across the room.

Don't model yelling and talking over people to your students if you don't want them to yell and talk over you.

Instead, be the change you want to see in your classroom. Model the behaviors that are congruent with your beliefs about teaching, learning, environment, relationships...

This example may seem extreme to you, but I witnessed it. The teacher could not see how to be the change in his classroom. He was not open to hearing the hard truth. There was no moment of recognition and asking for help. Being the change you want in your classroom requires vulnerability and taking personal and professional responsibility for yourself. There will be times you need help. Asking for it will take courage. Receiving and implementing will take strength—perhaps beyond anything you've experienced before. But fountain teachers do it.

Being the change you want to see in your classroom can be daunting or magical. It depends on how open to making a difference you really are. If you are willing and open, you can overcome the difficult parts and move to the magic more easily than a teacher who pays only lip service to the desire, but continues to fortify her defensive position. What is your level of commitment to being this change?

Here are some action steps to consider as you contemplate sharing your fountain ways by being the change you want to see in your classroom. If these actions are congruent with your vision of great teaching, take them on. If these actions are congruent, yet you run into some dissonance between your current practices and these actions, jump into the wrestling ring with that discomfort. Don't overlook it. Honestly open each issue and ask yourself what you have to do in order to come into alignment between your current practices and these actions. If these actions are not congruent with your vision of great teaching, make a list that is. Then go through the exercise of checking your current actions against your list. Here is a mini list of mine to get you started.

- Be fully present.
- Listen while your students are talking.
- Stop multitasking and engage.

- Greet your students at the classroom door
- Be prepared each day. Do not spend your morning time running around, trying to prep for the day, while getting the students in the door.

To be the change in your classroom, try this on for size: make the decision and take the action to arrive at school five minutes early. When you are fully aware and in tune, five minutes can seem like an hour. You can change the entire flow of your day by arriving five minutes early, especially when you get your classroom systems in order. Get systemized and organized. Then, when the bell rings, you can be at the door to greet your students and invite them into a classroom where learning takes place. This is a great practice. Preparation and welcoming your students impact learning in powerful ways.

In her work on shame and vulnerability, Dr. Brene Brown discovered that all we humans really want is to know we've been seen and heard and that we matter. This desire begins early in our lives. It is not something that appears when you reach forty. For teachers, Dr. Brown's research opens a critical door of understanding. If this is what our students crave, then let's take the opportunity at the beginning of each day to meet this need. Being the change you want to see in your classroom could mean recognizing each child, hearing each child, and letting each one know that he or she matters. Your level of preparedness shows how much they matter. Make no mistake; this action speaks volumes. Get intentional about how children enter your classroom. Greet each one with a handshake, a hug, a high-five, or a smile. Set your classroom environment intentionally. *Create* your classroom environment. Do not allow *reaction* to set the tone for your classroom.

By *creating*—being intentional, establishing your vision, and modeling the behaviors you want to see in your classroom—you are sharing great teaching with the students in your classroom. This is it! This is where the legacy begins. When children are seen, heard, and know they matter through all the intentional actions you do throughout the

day, lives change. Sharing starts right in your classroom with your students. Be the change you want to see in your classroom.

Share: Be the Change You Want to See in Your School

Sharing does not end in your classroom. The second stone in our bag of Sharing is *Be the change you want to see in your school*. Here you step out of the isolated environment that you create in your classroom. You recognize that you are part of a larger community. You are part of your school. Great teachers have the responsibility to share their philosophies and to lead the way. You recognize that vision and intention are life-changers. Great teachers look forward to sharing their work with their colleagues. However, you also recognize that actions are the fragrance that draws people to the fountain—not words.

In order to share in your school, you must be the change you want to see in your school. Start with yourself. Examine your behaviors. What do you model? How do you conduct yourself in the hallway? What do your colleagues see? How do you interact with others in public? Remember, most people don't get to come in your classroom. They won't see the brilliance of your classroom work firsthand. They will feel the ripple effects of it through your students, but the direct experience of your fountain ways will be saved for your students, unless you set the intention to be the change you want to see in your school.

For this reason, your actions outside of your classroom are as important as your actions in your classroom. Consider the person who teaches next door to you. Do you really know how she or he works? Do you really know how she or he manages the classroom and the students in it? All you really have is your impression of this person from when she or he is present in public spaces. Likewise, that's all that other people have of you: their impression of you in public spaces.

So what do you model? When you are in an assembly, do you grade papers? Are you texting and checking e-mail? Are you making out your grocery list? Or are you fully engaged with the speaker or event? Do you recognize the opportunity to learn and grow in any situation? I've been witness to teachers over the years that bring stacks of papers to student assemblies, who text during programs and performances, and who write lesson plans during faculty meetings. These behaviors are not congruent with the fountain overflow of joy that comes from being authentically, 100 percent present.

Is the Multi-tasker a Great Fountain Teacher?

No matter if a motivational speaker, an awards assembly with or without parent involvement, or an afternoon faculty meeting, if you're not fully attending to the person or event, what is the message you are sending to your colleagues (not to mention the performer/speaker/ host)? Take a moment to answer. Don't gloss over this one.

Now let's flip the situation. Let's say you are fully attending. You are highly engaged with what is happening. You are showing your joy and authenticity for the moment, event, speaker, or meeting. You are open to the new idea because you might learn something that makes you more successful or your students more successful. Now what are you modeling to your colleagues and to the student body at large? Being authentically and fully engaged in the moment is a beautiful thing. Take a minute to consider the difference between the two scenarios. Which example gives you more opportunity to share your beliefs and to be the change you want to see in your school?

In addition to sharing with your school family through moment-to-moment engagement, fountain teachers also share this work in another way. This time, our model is important, but our engagement is changing. Instead of participating through observing and receiving, now we move to standing up for our clearly defined beliefs and helping to bring others to the realization of our intentions to change lives through education.

There will be times when you will have to question ideas, mandates, or processes. You'll reflect on your beliefs and on the new information, and you'll ask yourself, "In the filter of my belief system, how does this 'new thing' fit?" and "Do I really think this is a good idea?" You may not agree with what you are hearing. This situation will require you to question the program and process. You will have to work to find pieces, parts, or a new angle to the thing that you are being asked to do. In some way, you'll have to assimilate part of this "new thing" so that you can work with it. Lean on your new mantra: "I am willing to see things differently."

In another situation, you may hear the new idea and know immediately that it is a match to your beliefs. You may be ready to jump onboard and implement instantly.

Whichever situation you find yourself in, you have a responsibility to share your beliefs. Fountain teachers have clear visions and can communicate their beliefs and vision to others. Sharing the clarity of your vision and your thought-provoking questions, asked from a place of love (fountain teachers are not pot-stirrers) will cause those around you to question their own beliefs and to wonder how they feel about teaching. This is a great beginning for sharing your work in the world. You are being the change you want to see in your school.

Why is Sharing this Work So Important?

Consider this: besides the sheer number of students in the world and the fact that any one person alone cannot teach them all, there are also some children in this world that you are not meant to reach. They are not an energetic match for you. You care about them. You see them as important. You want them to be seen, heard, and know that they matter, but you are not the match for them. One of your colleagues is.

Yes, sometimes a student belongs with someone else. This is one more reason we must be the change we want to see in our school. If we want the best for all the children and we recognize that we aren't the exact match for every one of them, then we also must realize that our colleagues need access to the principles of the Great Fountain Teachers. In the world of the fountain teacher, cooperation and support rule. Competition among colleagues does not exist. Fountain teachers recognize there is plenty of success to go around and the success felt by one can be shared by many. Fountain teachers are not in competition with the person in the room next door or across the hall.

I've taught with teachers who wouldn't share anything and with teams of teachers that shared everything. The quality of the work coming from the sharing team was much superior to what any one of us could do alone. Folks who do not want to share are teaching from a mind-set of lack. They won't share because they're afraid that somebody else will get one up on them. This is the burned-out, scared candle teacher. She's saying, "I am only going to last a little longer. I cannot share my success. I can't tell people how to do what I do, because then they're going to get some of the glow off of my flame." This is not the confident teacher focused on the greatness of the collective whole who serves from her overflow.

You are a fountain. You share from overflow. You know there is abundance. You know that every child deserves what you believe in, and so you feel compelled to share your best with every teacher. You recognize the teacher across the hall has a gift for sharing with particular students that you can't reach. You must share with your colleagues because you know you can't reach all students. Collections of teachers are needed.

Share by overflowing. You don't push others into your work. You do not pull them into this work kicking and screaming but, by serving and sharing from your overflow, others will question you and will want a piece of your authenticity, joy, and success. You share and make a difference with your colleagues by knowing your beliefs, by having clear visions, by questioning, by articulating your perspective, and by reaching out to others in love. These behaviors make a difference. I promise you they do.

When you embrace this type of sharing, something else wonderful will happen. People will begin to notice, and they will be drawn to you. Remember the beauty, tranquility, and promise of hope that a fountain possesses are what draws people to it. You are this fountain.

Be ready. Your colleagues will recognize a difference in you. They will begin to seek answers from you. They will be interested in what you have to say. Acknowledge this. Be ready to take on the next level of leadership. You will not only lead from the ranks, but you will be put in the position to mentor. This does not have to happen formally. It does not necessarily mean a brand-new position coming your way. It may mean afternoon chats with the teacher next door. It can be that easy and that powerful! Reaching another teacher in the quiet moments of the afternoon can rock worlds. This time of day can leave us ultra-vulnerable. Be sure to engage with this seeking colleague carefully.

Before leaving this aspect of being the change you want to see in your school, I want you to consider one more of the benefits of sharing with your colleagues. When you step up to share your beliefs, whether from the ranks or as a mentor to another, it solidifies what you know. Think about what it takes to teach something. You must understand a concept before you can teach it, but remember that teaching the concept will also impact your understanding of it. So, be willing to show up as a fountain and to share your overflow with others. Remember not to drown your bystanders but to refresh them so that they will come back repeatedly for a little more each time.

Share: Be the Change You Want to See in the World

You get the idea behind sharing. You are actually sharing by being the change you want both in your classroom and in your school. But you know your work does not end in your school. Fountain teachers think globally. The world gets smaller every day. Your opportunities to interact with people from across the globe are vast and growing. You no longer live, work, and play only in your part of the world. The Internet has connected us. There is no turning back.

You may ask, "How can I be the change in the world when I am only one?" I would pose it to you another way: "How can I not be the change in the world when I am one?"

To begin the ripple effect, it only takes one small pebble. Flow where you are and remember when the teacher is ready, the student will appear. If you are open to mentoring one person in your school, then you are no longer a lone pebble. You are now a rock band.

But to overflow to the world, go online. The world is literally at your fingertips. How can you share with teachers around the world? Get on Pinterest, join Facebook, sign up for Google Plus, develop a professional page on LinkedIn, or start tweeting. Additionally, look up education bloggers and join their conversations. You can find my blog at www.BeeSharp.us/articles. Leave comments. Share your opinions. Heck, start your own blog! Put your voice into the world. Don't want to be in the mainstream social networks? Join with me in the International Academy of Bee Sharp Teachers. We have a private forum for member teachers only. You are safe with us.

When you begin to seek opportunity to share with the world, you will be amazed at what you'll find. Admittedly, some of it will be junk, but some will be wonderful, compelling conversation that will provoke you to lean into your beliefs, share yours with passion, or even tweak your thoughts. When I first started interacting with teachers around the world, I realized that many of our issues are the same. Oh sure, there are differences, but lots of teachers feel the stress of standardized testing. To varying degrees folks also feel stressed by the overbearing parent and the under-involved parent. Lack of materials and disparity in funding amounts rank high across the board among teachers' issues.

Common themes such as these were the reason I took the Academy of Bee Sharp Teachers international. I realized that even on opposite sides of the globe, teachers had many things in common and could help each other. I also realized that the message of personal and professional empowerment for women is an international issue. We must support each other.

The individual steps to becoming the fountain may look different for each person across the globe, but the stones in each bag used to build the path are the same. We must all decide, believe, and share. So reach out. Take full advantage of the Internet. Connect with other teachers around the world. Investigate a class project that will engage your students in the lives of children around the world. Be willing to see things differently. Engage with the world or some new small part of it. The refreshing spray of the fountain teacher is meant to be shared.

Don't wait to be perfect or have it all figured out. Understand that sharing yourself as the change you want to see in the world starts with your open heart. No one expects perfection from you. We want your voice. We want your interaction, your guidance, your kindness, your story. We want you as the authentic you only you can be. Sharing and connecting in new ways can be scary, but the rewards are infinite. Start small and expand. Join me in the International Academy of Bee Sharp Teachers. This is a safe environment in which to begin your journey of sharing globally. Check it out: http://www.HowToBeAGreatTeacher.com

Section 3

There is only one way to avoid criticism: do nothing, say nothing, and be nothing.

Aristotle

Eight

THE SHIFT HITS THE FAN

Everything has beauty, but not everyone can see.

Confucius

Decide, Believe, Share

*Y*ou have before you three velvet bags, each embroidered with one of these words: Decide, Believe, and Share. These bags hold the stones that build the path to becoming a great fountain teacher. You have the nine-step framework here in this book. This is a lifetime of work, a journey of growth. Once you begin approaching your teaching with these nine principles in mind, you will never be or teach the same again. Your awareness has been prodded and poked; it cannot rest in dormancy. This is good news. Change has occurred. This is big stuff, important stuff, the stuff of a wonderful life. I am thrilled for you. I delight in the thought of you on your journey!

Keep in mind, however, as with all change, some growing pains will occur. Shifts will happen inside you and in your outer world. Be aware of this. You cannot expect to go deep within your belief system and not have change occur. Change may come in the form of losing old friends, gaining new ones, or both. New family dynamics may come into play. Your classroom may look, sound, and feel different. Any number of things can shift while you are going through this process, which, by the way, never ends. Some shifts you will welcome wholeheartedly. Others will come with a price that you'd like to negotiate. At times, negotiation will not be an option. I don't want to be a Debbie Downer, but sometimes the shift will hit the fan.

Be Aware and Prepared

The point is to expect uncomfortable shifts to occur. Embrace them. When you honor your teaching, when you bring your authenticity into the classroom, when you teach with joy and success, when you are that kind of teacher, some people will not like it. They will wonder about this new person. Who is she? Where did this perspective come from? Why is the status quo not good enough anymore? Why aren't we compatible complainers? Even inside of yourself, you may hear the old voices saying, "We used to do it like this," or "Look at the teacher next door to you—she's staying later, she's taking a bigger bag home with her; she must be a better teacher." You're going to hear a lot of junk, both from within and from without.

Be strong, dear friend. Be aware that shifting mindsets can feel like sand in your swimsuit. Recognize when it does. Deal with it head-on by acknowledging it, questioning it using your five whys, applying your new mantra ("I am willing to see things differently"), and making conscious choices to create the life you want around it. If you need to cry over it, shout it out, or laugh in its face, do so, but then let it go. Send the gremlins away in peace and let go of them as they leave. Don't tell them to leave and then drag them back by their ankles. When you dismiss the old ideas, the old fears, the old doubts, and the self-sabotage, let them go freely. Untie the thin tether you secretly hold—the "just in case" rope. Let go. You don't need the false security of your old candle ways. You are a fountain, ready to serve from your overflow.

You may already be feeling a bit of these shifts and noticing that there is a place of discomfort within your soul where your work of changing the paradigm has begun. That's great! Discomfort is a natural part of learning. It motivates us to search for solutions, because we want to relieve the pain. We persevere because we believe we can relieve the pain, solve the problem, or meet with a satisfying conclusion (and you can). Remember the third stone in the Believe bag: believe that you can do this work. Believing in you is part of being the fountain teacher. You can do this!

The Rub—There's a Real Name for It

The discomfort you feel is what I call the rub. It's the place from which we grow. There was a fellow by the name of Leon Festinger who came out with an official theory in 1957 that suggested we have an inner drive to hold all our attitudes and beliefs in harmony and avoid disharmony (or dissonance). His theory is called cognitive dissonance. According to Festinger, you experience cognitive dissonance when your beliefs and your behaviors are in conflict. You feel yucky. Therefore, in order to feel better, you change either your beliefs or your behaviors. This restores you to balance. The problem is, many people do this without consciousness. They simply react and reflex into something that doesn't hurt so bad. Take for example what happens when I go to the beach. I have a belief that walking is good for my health. So when I go to the beach, I start out to take a walk. A few steps in, I notice the sand rubbing between my thighs. It feels bad. I react and stop walking. I want to walk because I believe it is good for my health, but the sand makes it rub and feel bad so I don't do it. This is unconscious reaction mode.

In contrast, the way fountain teachers deal with cognitive dissonance—the rub—is by consciously making decisions backed by actions, examining their beliefs, and sharing their change with others.

For you, fountain teacher, it may sound something like this: you feel in your heart and soul, "I want to be a nurturing, loving teacher who helps students learn deeply through exploration and creation of knowledge, but in order to get my kids to pass the test, I give my students packets of prep materials filled with multiple choice questions." This creates the rub. But you do not remain there. Your ability to move from dissonance to congruence in mind, spirit, and action is an essential differentiator for the fountain teacher.

First, decide to come to a place of congruence and take actions that support your decision. Relieve the rub. Second, dig into your beliefs and find the opportunities to mesh your beliefs with your actions (the five whys/your new mantra). Finally, talk out the issues and get support. Share your experience with others. This is your work.

Every stone you have pulled from your Decide, Believe, and Share bags exists to build your path to being the fountain. Revisit the principles outlined by the stones often. Check in with yourself, keeping honesty and curiosity as your guides. Fountain teachers do not stand in judgment of their selves. As you examine your work and your life, ask, "Isn't that interesting?" This question will keep you from putting judgment on yourself. Questions like "Wasn't that dumb?" or "Why do I do such foolish things?" are full of judgment and do not belong in the repertoire of a fountain teacher.

So far in this chapter, you have seen that you will feel discomfort as you grow. You know that some folks will support you, but others will not. You knew this from the beginning. Remember, we talked about how your fountain spray will sometimes create mud as it hits the ground around it. You have also learned in this chapter that you will need to let go in peace, both of the unsupportive people and of your unsupportive inner voices. You will let them go and not hold onto them. This may sound like all of our great fountain work leads to isolation, but that is not true. Some folks will receive your spray as the grass receives the water. You will nourish them, and they will come to you for more. As you become clear about your beliefs, you will be able to recognize others who feel the same way as you and make conscious decisions to spend your time with these folks. Also, people with similar beliefs will be able to recognize your beliefs now because they are clear. Previous to this work, others could not tell what you believed because your unconscious actions and reactions clouded your mirror. Now that you have rubbed your mirror clean, free of the haze of confusion, folks who have similar beliefs will be drawn to you. They will see in your mirror a reflection that fits their image.

Enlist a Team to Support You

Additionally, you will develop and become a member of a tribe who will support you. This can start with your family. They love you. Whether your family is a spouse, children, parents, dogs, cats...You matter to them. Begin by intentionally enlisting them as part of your support team. Share with them that you are changing and need their help. When I explained to my family that I needed to be 100 percent at work when working so that I could be 100 percent at home when I was at home, they gave me a half-hearted OK. But when my actions began to support this, they got onboard, and yours will too. People love when they have 100 percent of you, when you are fully present with them. So speak to your family about the intentions you are setting and your focus on showing up fully in your life. When you need to give full focus to a project, tell your family this. Then, when it is full family-focus time, tell them and live your intention. When they understand what you are doing and begin reaping the benefits of your commitment to being fully present with them, they're going to support you more and more.

When this network of support is in place, you'll be able to withstand the tough times at school or anywhere in the world. Don't skimp on team training, though. Communicate with your family! Then rely on them to step up and support you. Expect their support, and they will meet your expectation. If you tell them what you need and don't allow them to live up to it, you are essentially setting them up for failure. It won't work. Be clear about what you need and give them manageable steps. Grow them into this new way of living at the pace that works. Slow and fast do not matter. Living with supported ease does.

Having a home network of support is wonderful. But support does not stop there. The principle of sharing as outlined in this book puts an emphasis on you being what you want to see in your classroom, your school, and the world. But you see and feel that you need a support network—folks who can hold you up in the rough moments. So your support network begins at home and then grows outward. Find someone in your building, in your school district, or in an Internet group that shares your beliefs. Engage in regular communication with them that affirms your beliefs. Share your fountain work with them. Having the support at home is essential to this work, but having a support system of colleagues—either in your locale or virtually through the Internet—is also critical. Join us in the International Academy of Bee Sharp Teachers. Our private members' site gives you a safe and secure place to get and give professional support (and share the love) with other folks who are like you, passionate about teaching with authenticity, joy, and loads of success. Like honeybees in a colony, individual bees cannot survive for long alone.

Nine

CONVOCATION

Whatever the mind of man can conceive and believe, it can achieve.

Napoleon Hill

Final Thoughts

As you near the end of this book, recognize you have only just begun the journey. You are not wrapping up the ideas and putting a finishing bow on them. You are actually taking your first steps toward becoming the fountain teacher. Your work is not of one small book to be read and discarded. This is the work of the rest of your life. You will revisit the principles held in this book repeatedly. You will come back here to reread sections at a time. You may even reread this entire book before the beginning of each school year, or at the close, to refresh your work during the summer season. Each time you revisit this book, it will enlighten you in a different way. This will happen because each time you come back to the pages, you will have grown while away. This material will not get old because you are ever-changing and bringing new perspective to the pages. Embrace this book as you would the hand of a dear friend. Throughout the years the hands age and show the work of life etched in the lines, crevices, knuckles, and nails. But the hand belongs to your friend. You embrace it in a gentle clasp, and it embraces you back—right where you are—with love and tenderness.

The reasons you do this work are so you can teach and live from your passion with joy and success and retire vibrantly filled with life and love. These are your moments right here, right now. Authenticity, joy, and success do not come at the end of a journey. It is the journey that provides us the opportunities to be authentic and experience joyful success. Success is not something you get on Tuesday, and then it's over. Success is something that you have daily, throughout your day, and throughout your life. It's based on the decisions you make and the belief you have in yourself that you can do this.

What you seek is seeking you.

Rumi

Decide now. Believe you can. Share your journey.

About The Author

Wynn Godbold once lived the life of the disappointed disillusioned teacher. She changed course by building a new path for herself as teacher, mom, wife, daughter—woman in the world. By living what she outlines in this book, she was able to teach in the midst of No Child Left Behind and various other education reforms that took place in the United States of America holding fast to her beliefs and was happy doing it.

Wynn is the founder of the International Academy of Bee Sharp Teachers and Bee Sharp Educator Training Associates, LLC. She is a dedicated speaker, trainer, and advocate who has taken her passion for teaching and life, and channeled it into an empowering movement for teachers everywhere.

Visit her at www.HowToBeAGreatTeacher.com to explore Bee Sharp TV and Wynn's in-depth, straight-talking video series on how to teach with overflow. Find out how you can be part of the movement to help teachers change the paradigm and bring the happy back into their classrooms and their lives.

Made in the USA
Middletown, DE
18 August 2019